1 MONTH OF
FREE
READING

at
www.ForgottenBooks.com

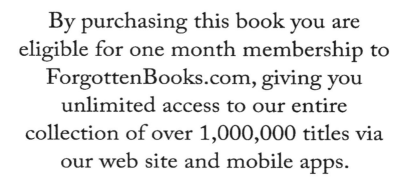

By purchasing this book you are eligible for one month membership to ForgottenBooks.com, giving you unlimited access to our entire collection of over 1,000,000 titles via our web site and mobile apps.

To claim your free month visit: www.forgottenbooks.com/free788927

ISBN 978-0-483-56867-9
PIBN 10788927

EDUCATION

BY

N. RUSSELL MIDDLETON,

AUTHOR OF

"*The Allegory of Plato and other Essays*
in Prose and Verse."

EDITED BY HIS SON,

N. R. MIDDLETON, Jr.

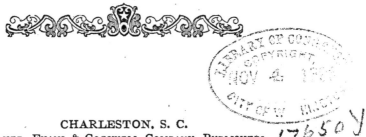

CHARLESTON, S. C.
WALKER, EVANS & COGSWELL COMPANY, PUBLISHERS,
3 and 5 Broad and 117 East Bay Streets,
1893.

"Fellow-man" of the Author,

THIS VOLUME IS DEDICATED

PREFACE.

Not until after arranging the Essays which constitute this volume, for publication in their present form, did I determine upon the name of the Book. I had placed that on "Education" at the beginning, and, as the succeeding Essays are extentions, demonstrations and amplifications of the first, its name seemed not an inappropriate title to the volume.

EDITOR.

The attention of the reader is called to the following typographical errors:

Page	Line		
11	18	Read ; after failures for ,	
55	1	"	Vasa for Vassa.
68	10	"	ambiguous for ambiguou.
162	1	"	skilful for skllful.
233	9	"	Christ for Chris.
234	16	"	troubles for roubles.

TABLE OF CONTENTS.

EDUCATION.

Among enlightened nations the subject of Education becomes every day more important, men are beginning to feel,—they have been brought by the most startling and disastrous experiences to feel—that it is fundamental, that it lies at the root, not only of individual, but of social and national prosperity. Nor has this been a barren or fruitless persuasion; vast sums have been expended, vigorous efforts have been exerted, and heroic sacrifices have been endured in the cause of education. Governments have included it within the scope of their responsibility, and high-minded men have consecrated their accumulations to its diffusion. It is well that this should be so; it is well that the development of mind and character should keep pace, to some extent, at least, with commercial enterprise and material aggrandizement, for assuredly the refinements of civilization would afford no permanent or real advantage if they did not involve in their progress both mental and moral culture.

But while there is no difference of opinion upon this point, while all thinking men agree as to the necessity for education, there are scarcely any two who are of one mind as to the object and the mode.   I desire to say a few words upon this interesting topic, and, as scientific investigation necessarily involves intelligent division, I propose to consider the question under three heads : The *subject*, the *method* and the *result*, and I invoke, in aid of the discussion, that superhuman wisdom which it plainly demands.

The *subject*, a rational being ; a being created for moral purposes, and ushered into existence under such a condition of equilibrium between two opposing elements, as to leave the choice in his own hands, and thus make him the real arbiter of his own destiny.

The metaphysical enquiries connected with the freedom of the will, its nature and extent, do not affect the present question ; whoever is disposed to deny the postulate is at liberty to try the experiment and act, if he sees fit, as an irrational and irresponsible being, but all intelligent intercourse between human beings presupposes moral responsibility, and it is a mere waste of time, in a serious discussion, to attempt to prove it.

But while this characteristic of humanity is generally acknowledged, it is not always appreciated or understood. There are those who look upon their moral status and the difficulties which it involves as a gratuitous and arbitrary exertion of divine power, instituted wholly in the interest of the divine honor, and in furtherance of the divine aggrandizement. This is simply the application of our human experience to superhuman conditions of existence; it is a transference of finite necessities to infinite being; it is undertaking to speak of the absolute from assumed analogies in the relative; it is all pure assumption, and contrary to the real probabilities of the case.

There is no *want* in the Deity; he has no needs, nor personal desires, nor personal interests of any kind to consult; he cannot, by any automatic act of his creatures, be made either greater or happier than he is, self-love can have no place in his consciousness, because there is no room for its presence, and no field for its exercise. The thoughts, provisions and affections of the Deity are, from the necessity of the case, wholly objective ; his being is one continual efflux of power, issuing in existence, both mental and material ; one of the forms of that existence—the form which it assumes in the personality of man—is moral life—life imparted with certain limitations, and for certain purposes ; attached to that life is such a freedom of will as is necessary to indicate the character and fix the status of responsible intelligences ; a freedom limited by the necessity of the case, and enjoyed by permission ; not absolute, but defined and appropriated.

Such is man, an intelligent agent, in perfect equilibrium between good and evil, and free therefore to choose between them. What more than this can man require, not only for perfect contentment with his lot, but for gratitude and exultation in accepting it ?

Let us bring the question to a practical test ; let observation and experience vindicate the benignity of the Creator in the moral department of his creation ; what do we see in looking around us ? What do we feel forever within ? The ceaseless pressure of life upon the limitations which encompass it; man every where struggling, discontented, seeking higher and better things for himself ; beating against his prison bars or madly at strife with his fellow under a vague impression of hinderance from without, seeking rest and finding none. And why is it that he finds no rest? Why is it that in the midst of this limitless creation, surrounded by countless ministrations of good, with every appetite gratified and every passion appropriately provided for, there is never, for one solitary moment of his progressive existence, a pause of satisfaction, a wayside inn, a bower of repose? Is there no significance in the fact that the policemen of time are ever at hand, in the crowded thoroughfare, to urge on the loiterer and compel him to advance. Does this sense of pressure, this restless turning of the giant under the superincumbent weight of the actual give no hint of his true nature and his ultimate destiny? Why is it that, surrounded by all the appliances of wealth and all the satisfactions of power and all the enticements of luxury, man turns his back resolutely upon the whole and seeks liberty and expansion in arctic snows or tropical deserts, thankful to escape from inertia by grappling even with death ?

The answer has been given by a thousand tongues, in a thousand forms, in prose and in poetry, in science and in song ; but it is ever the same unfaltering reply : there is in man something higher than man ; a superhuman consciousness inspires, a superhuman energy impels him, and he can never rest until the craving of his higher nature has been satisfied, and the constituents of his being have been crystalized into a higher form of unity and beauty : man has been introduced into relative and circumscribed existence, not as a finality, not as the true sphere of his development and the ultimate scope of his powers, but simply as a condition of preliminary training, and the moment he regards it as an end, the moment he limits his responsibilities and his satisfactions by material and relative considerations, he descends from his allotted platform, forfeits his appointed rank and surrenders the patent of his true nobility. Let him not then decline for a moment the struggle which awaits him, let him not consent to surrender his birth-

right for any pressure either of fear or desire, let not
any mock humility or false modesty shelter him from
the disgrace of sinking, in indolence and cowardice,
the glories of his magnificent inheritance. He is
man; it is well that he should remember his native
destitution, but it is at his peril that he forgets his
inherited grandeur. (Standing as he does midway
between heaven and hell; centering in his personality
their infinite antagonism; suspending upon his will
their eternal issues; giving audience to their ministers
and passing judgment upon their claims; what is
there, what can there be, among created intelligences,
higher than a moral being conscious of his morality
and recognizing its true significance? Said one, upon
whose oracular deliverances I once hung with breath-
less attention (and I wish I could repeat his very
words, for there was in them a force which I cannot
hope to impart), " I never saw an angel; I know
nothing experimentally of those superhuman intelligences; but I have seen a man, and I have no words
to express the grandeur of that sight; alone in the
midst of enemies; revilers and detractors all
around; every weapon, that petty malice could invent

or malignant hate supply, discharged against him; friends debauched; foes triumphant; he stood, calm amidst the uproar, unquivering, unblenching, the master of the storm. It was man but it was something more than man, and I bowed before a spirit in which the Deity had manifestly taken up his abode."

I have no controversy with those who love to dwell upon the other side of the picture. If, in any case, there is a felt necessity for humiliation, if, by a weak and unauthorized act of appropriation, man forgets, in the contemplation of his powers, the source from which he has derived them and becomes insolent and wanton, it may be necessary, in very kindness, to pluck from him his borrowed robes and leave him, for a time, to his native destitution. But this is after all but a half truth and needs a supplement to make it perfect, for while mortification and shame may stimulate to effort, it is self-respect alone that can grasp possession; it is not when I think of my human limitations, but when I remember my divine extraction, that I can claim with confidence a royal inheritance, and of this I am well assured, that it is when I best appreciate the nobility of that inheritance, that I most thoroughly recognize my **own** shortcoming.

We are shocked at the sight of human degrada-tion ; the Neros and Caligulas, the Borgias and deMontforts of history seem to involve, both in their origin and their end, a malignant influence ; but why are we shocked? Why do we utter an involuntary protest against these monsters and disavow them as the exponents of their race ? Why do we instinctively and peremptorily point to another picture, illustrating, for our encouragement, the records of the Solons and the Platos, the Oberlins and the Fenelons, whose lives and persons seem to shroud, by an almost trans-parent veil, the lineaments of divinity ? Why is it, that through the long lapse of intervening ages, not one solitary voice has ever dared to lift itself in calumny against the divine man to whom we are permitted to point as the exponent of our wills and the true type of our race? It is from a divine intuition ; it is because man is conscious of harboring a germ of immortality, and knows that he is responsible for its nurture, and while he feels the pressure, is alive to the honor of that responsibility. Yes ! we may sink into sensuality if we will; we may suffer ourselves to be overpowered by the delusions of this relative and phenomenal existence; we may struggle for tinsel crowns and vanishing possessions and servile power; but there is a protest going on within which proclaims our paternity and demands our inheritance.

If these things are so, then the *method* of our Education must be in accordance with the truth which they imply, that is, a method which recognizes the true nature of man, his origin and his end; anything short of this must end in ultimate failure. To educate man as if three score years and ten were the boundary of his existence, as if the satisfactions of his phenomenal life were the limit of his enjoyment and the measure of his duty, would result in a collapse involving the very interests we were endeavoring to promote; it is as impossible to secure these minor interests without reference to the greater as it would be to apprehend locomotion without space or succession without duration. The metaphysical distinction of Cousin between the logical and chronological order of sequence applies in its full force to the philosophy of education. Secure in your subject the principles of truth, honor, virtue and accountability, and you have a solid foundation for success in any field of human development in which his efforts may be expended; give a man true views of his maker, let him know what he has to fall back upon when his own virtue fails him, his own power is exhausted and his social experiences have sickened him with life and made him an abhorrence to himself, and you bring at once into active and beneficent operation the virtues of patience, courage, industry and perseverence, which lie at the root of all success, whether in the nurture of a plant or the acquirement of a profession, whether in the solution of a problem or the government of a nation. This want of thoroughness, this inability to face the truth, this horror in the presence of absolute verities, which exhibit themselves on every side, are the cause of all our disastrous failures, temporary success, immediate practical results, low aims and narrow views drag down to the level of the actual the nature which was formed to converse with the real, and the shouts of a thoughtless multitude are accepted as the utterance of a divine sanction.

But the process through which the moral being must pass on to its perfection is a very different one from this, its defects are radical and so must be the remedy; the warfare between the lower and the higher nature is internecine; from the very nature of the case there can be no compromise, material interests and sensual passions weigh like lead upon the spirit and bind its powers and check its aspirations, until it ceases to assert itself and withdraws from the discouraging contest. It is manifest then, that the field of this deadly encounter cannot be a bed of roses; the very condition upon which it is occupied is a condition of trial, and the severity of the test is in proportion to the magnitude of the result. Is it in accordance with any analogy, human or divine, that a created being should rise into a higher form of existence without effort, without an experience in which energies and agonies are inevitably involved?

Trial! why the very machinery of human industry, the very machinery of human production must be subjected to trial; you cannot discharge a rifle or wield a sword or fill a boiler, until you have proved their qualities by a maximum test; and in the higher walks of life, upon the loftier platform of intelligent existence, shall the agent march unchallenged into the field of his operations? Shall he give no account of his powers, and acknowledge no responsibility for his freedom? Is it nothing that we are capable of honor, that we can apprehend truth, that we can attain to purity, and shall we be required to give no proof of our estimate of these priceless qualities? Indeed it is difficult to imagine how we could either appropriate or display them, if there were no background of difficulty to project them upon the canvass. It is at this point and under these conditions that man is permitted to appropriate his virtue; it is his, not by inherent right, not by actual possession, not by perfect practice, but by a choice under difficulties; a choice put to the severest test and maintained under the severest pressure that his nature is capable of enduring. Here lies the solution of the moral problem, the clue to the labyrinth of moral existence, which the Theseus—the true hero—accepts and retains until "death is swallowed up in victory."

What then is the *result?* It grows naturally and inevitably out of the antecedents. A moral being, who has been introduced by the appropriate education of of his powers into the higher forms of spiritual life, must, from the necessity of the case, become noble and glorious. A man, who by the reception and cultivation of divine influences in his nature has resisted the enticements of sense and the seductions of flattery and the frowns of power, has silently but effectually appropriated the constituents of immortality, Through whatever depths of misery he may have passed ; whatever defilements may have attached themselves to his outer garments ; however oppressed or neglected or despised he may have been in this relative condition of existence, he is absolutely noble ; he has taken up and absorbed into his being the elements of real life ; he is released from the seductions of the phenomenal and the entanglements of the relative, and become naturalized in the region of the real and the absolute ; and surely it is a glorious emancipation ; to have settled, once and forever, the relative value of things, to have organized existence by a fundamental and scientific classification, to have mastered, not only the logic of words and the logic of ideas, but the logic of facts and the logic of events ;

to have assigned their appropriate place and affixed their real value to the apparently discordant elements of our perplexing experience ; to understand the non-entity of the apparent, the vanity of the transitory, and the feebleness of the derived; to stand thus, in the simple consciousness of a divine affiliation, and look through the apparent to the real source of safety and power; I do not see what more can be demanded by a rational being conscious of imperfection and struggling to shake it off.

VIRTUE.

Virtue—Manhood—Courage—and is it not fitly named? Who, that has made any efforts towards self-culture and self-purification, can fail to see the beauty and the appropriateness of the term, as applied to the development and exercise of our higher nature? and who, that has had any experience of the result of those efforts, can cease to be grateful, that he has been permitted and required to make them.

The sense of victory, in such a contest as is implied in the struggle with our selfish passions, is, in itself, an ample reward for all the trials it involves; but, when there is superadded the consequences of that victory; when we come to realize, not only victory, but advance, and that advance in our very nature itself, that we actually are higher and nobler beings than we were, living a higher life, breathing a purer air, unaffected by that which once annoyed, and uninfluenced by that which once allured us, it will require no effort, either of mind or will, to apply to the process the most exalted term which our vocabulary can furnish. It is a matter for which, I think, we have cause to congratulate ourselves, that the word, which has been adopted to express our highest exaltation, is one which, at the same time, affirms and challenges our true nobility.

We do not speak of human rectitude as angelic or divine; when we use these terms we intend to speak hyperbolically, but we call it virtue—manhood; and I rejoice that it is so; I rejoice that human nature, with all its degraded propensities, can still maintain its conscious nobility, and recognize its grand responsibility.

In every age of the world it has been so, and in the most degraded forms of humanity; a standard of some kind is established, and that standard always involves effort, struggle, for the maintenance of which courage is needed, and the exercise of that courage is virtue. In the savage it is the triumph over his physical nature, in the endurance of pain, and the defiance of death, for his personal protection and comfort. Ascending a step higher in the scale of civilization, we find friendship and patriotism the motives of virtue, as was the case among the Greeks and Romans, until we come, in Christian ethics, to self-abnegation, in consideration of the needs of sentient existence in every department of creation ; virtue, in that system, being understood to imply the possession and exercise of all those qualities which constitute the perfection of rational existence.

It would, at first, seem strange, that the Christian standard should have any use for a word, which expresses manhood in the lower forms of human development ; in other words, that it should require any courage to practice virtue, in the Christian sense of the term.

Experience, however, soon convinces us of its appropriateness, and not only so, but, that the courage is in accordance with the virtue, that it is as far above all other courage, as the virtue is above other virtue.

Think of the isolation, of the misapprehension, of the misrepresentation ; think of the severe mental pressure involved in the nice distinctions which a sense of duty demands ; think of the heart-sickening consciousness of terrible shortcomings, and of the over-

whelming advantage which those shortcomings afford
to the unprincipled and the censorious; think of the
tremendous difficulty involved in the distinction between humility and self-abasement, between self-respect and pride, between firmness and obstinacy;
think of present, pressing, palpable necessity and the
dim vision of a supply escaping in the distance from
the arms of a relaxing faith; think of being sent alone
and unarmed, to march, with a hostile banner through
an armed and irritated mob; and then talk about
worldly heroes and worldly courage. Think of the
loneliness, of the entire lack of encouragement, of
sympathy, of applause. How powerful and palpable
must be the apprehension of a higher life, and of a
divine presence, to enable us to stand, for one moment, under the neglect, the disapproval, the contempt
of the wise and the respectable and the powerful
around us; to feel, that in uttering our solemn convictions, and in meeting our unavoidable responsibilities, we are underlying the old insinuated sneer,
"what will this babbler say?" or, if the utterance, be
too true and too powerful to be questioned, then to
encounter that other stealthy thrust, "we know this

fellow whence he is." Nor is this the utmost extent
of the trial, to which virtue is necessarily subjected;
all this is only external, it does not touch our true
life, and it affects us, only so far as we are under
worldly and selfish influences; but the conviction that
we cannot take refuge from it in conscious rectitude,
that the charge is, after all, only too true, that there
is, in fact, a very wide distinction between the truth
and its vehicle, between the profession and the practice, that not only have others just ground of dis-
satisfaction with us, but that, if we are honest, we must
be deeply dissatisfied with ourselves, that, after all,
in establishing and proclaiming our standard, we are
inevitably exposing our own short-coming; all this
presents itself to the mind of the honest enquirer
after truth, as a reality which must be met, and not
as a charge to be refuted, or a difficulty to be avoided.

This is fundamental; it affects the springs of our
existence; it poisons the fountain. Be the charges
of others what they may, we are not true to our own
standard, we do not live in accordance with our own
sense of right and wrong. Human sagacity is foiled,
and human wisdom confounded by such a presentation

as this, and we are shut up to an alternative that decides our destiny. Nothing is left but blank despair on the one hand, and divine interposition on the other. Two questions then present themselves for decision.

Has the Deity interposed for our relief?

What is the nature of His interposition?

In the investigation which naturally follows, the prominent criterion would be, the perfection of the remedy proposed. It would be the first and most conclusive test, applied to any system of theology claiming a divine origin. This indispensable criterion I do not find in any of the ancient Eastern systems; they, one and all, fall short in the character of the being, whom they represent as controlling the universe. I do not feel that I could safely entrust any one of them with the interests of my higher nature. There is too much vengeance and too much anthropomorphism in the Hebrew Jehovah, and the unity of the Moslem Allah is one with which a pure spiritual existence has but little in common. I turn to Christianity, and I am perfectly satisfied. I accept the conditions, I recognize the authority, I acknowledge the purity, I verify the truth and I rejoice in the paternity of the God, whom Jesus Christ has revealed as the Being in whom I live and move and have my being.

There is no mystery here; nothing which is not perfectly clear, and perfectly in accordance with my reason and my spiritual requirements. When I am told authoritatively, that I have an infinite Father, the questions which perplex my existence are set at rest forever. It covers the whole ground of my otherwise inexplicable existence, when I am assured, that a being of infinite perfection holds towards me the relationship, so imperfectly typified by the tenderness of human paternity.

And when I go farther, and look upon the mode he has adopted for my relief, I am equally satisfied. My individuality is respected, my identity is secured, my self-respect is consulted, my affections are cherished and elevated, my aspirations are answered, my conscience is set at rest, and I am separated from evil, not by an arbitrary decree which would unman me, but by a change in my nature, dependent upon my own cöoperation, which raises me above it.

I do not find, in the conditions upon which my acceptance turns, any subtle diplomacy or entangling casuistry, a single element of discord, or the most distant hint of antagonism with my race. In the ordering of a matter of such infinite moment, my nature demands simplicity and certainty—I find them both—"Be ye holy." "Without me ye can do nothing." "Come unto me." "Ask and ye shall receive." "The holy spirit shall guide you into all truth." "If ye, being evil, know how to give good gifts unto your children, how much more shall your Father which is in heaven give the holy spirit to them that ask?" I do not really see what more I could demand, consistently with the indispensable freedom of my will. Exerting my imagination to its utmost stretch, I cannot suggest any condition of existence which I would be willing to substitute for that in which I find myself placed by the Author of my being. In moments of despondency I may sigh for temporary relief, but I know very well, that I would not accept it upon the conditions, under which, alone, it could be afforded; and I know equally well, that, in the worst condition to which I may be reduced, I have been furnished with a resource, whose foundation is deeper than the lowest possible depths of human experience. Once establish for me a claim upon infinite power, and then, let finite evil do its worst. If my Creator has spoken to me; if he has assured me of this by a clear and direct communication, which I possess and apprehend, I am not at all careful to discuss or explain the subtle casuistries of human interpretations. I decline all invitations into the field of polemics, and content myself with the simple and narrow path of faith in the power and love of my protector and my guide.

I have no ability and no desire to understand or to explain his nature and his attributes, it is enough for me, that he is able and willing to help me, and that he has told me so himself; and if I am asked, what assurance I have, that this conviction is true, I answer, the same assurance that the infant has, that there is milk in its mother's breast—the assurance of experience.

I believe that it is from wandering from the simplicity of faith, that discords and schisms have arisen among the professors of Christianity. It is from not distinguishing properly between matters of faith and matters of intellect, and from an unfounded reliance upon the deliverances of the human understanding, that questions have been raised, and tests have been applied, which are neither suggested by reason nor warranted by inspiration.

Undoubtedly everything depends upon what sort of a God we believe in, but the practical value of the enquiry turns, not upon the constitution of the divine existence, which is wholly out of our reach and above our comprehension, and which is all comprised for us in the word, God—infinite good—, but upon his attitude and his relationship to us; and while he has shrouded the first inquiry in impenetrable darkness, a darkness which mocks and stultifies those who enter it, he has condescended to the destitution of our created natures by answering the other so simply, that "he that runs may read." The intellect has its legitimate field, science in every department of human existence—the whole compass of creation is open to it, and by proper processes of induction, it can approach, step by step, to the point, where a legitimate synthesis will present truth in its perfect unity. But

2

faith has another province, and a different work; her method is, not induction, but intuition; her touchstone is, not logic, but inspiration; her cŏoperator is, not man, but God.

The subject may be presented, advantageously, in another light; we have viewed it positively; it admits of a strong negative consideration. We may take manhood, as opposed, first to childishness. The Apostle Paul suggests this view, when he says "when I became a man, I put away childish things;" whatever essentially and distinctively belongs to childhood; not purity, nor truth, nor innocence, nor guilelessness, nor trust, nor unsuspiciousness; these belong to childhood, but only because it is nearer to the source of being—nearer to the pure and perfect one, and, if we could put aside the self-assertion of manhood, and transfer to our heavenly Father the allegiance which children acknowledge to their earthly parent, we should still find abundant room for the exercise of all those qualities, which inhere in a loyal and trusting nature in every stage of its existence. But the tricks of childhood, the thoughtlessness, the irresponsibility, the vanity, the petty ambition, the pleasure-seeking, the materialism of childhood, those who call themselves men, who would resent the denial of their claim to manhood, ought, in all consistency and all fair dealing, to put away these, as utterly unworthy of their position and their claims. In this aspect of the case, virtue is opposed to childishness.

It is, also, opposed to *effeminacy*, as a distinctive quality—as representing those peculiar delicacies and incapacities which belong exclusively to the gentler sex. In many things we may imitate woman to our great advantage, but not in those refinements which she claims especially as woman, as the softening and conserving element of society. In dress, in our bodily and mental habits, in our social and industrial attitude, we must discard effeminacy if we would put on manhood, if we would be virtuous in the manly sense of the term.

Finally, it is opposed to brutality—to the indulgence and cultivation of our animal nature—to the vindictiveness, the obstinacy, the rage, the cunning, the cruelty which are the natural and characteristic qualities of the lower orders of creation : all who yield to the control of these and kindred passions have surrendered their distinctive quality of reason, and sunk, in consequence, to the level of the unrea‑soning brute. In the two former cases, there may be left a remnant of vitality, a spark which may be kindled into a flame, but in this last, the soul would seem to be dead, and, with the soul, of course, all manhood, all virtue.

HONOR.

Honor, I define to be "the recognition of right and wrong, irrespective of a penalty, and in accordance with the highest standard to which we can attain." I do not suggest the definition as complete or exhaustive, but as the one which presents the subject in the light best adapted to a rational enquiry, and, as the mode in which I desire to discuss the question implies single-mindedness at the outset, I shall assume certain positions as necessarily conceded.

In the first place, I shall not waste time in entering upon any discussion as to the nature of our existence ; I shall take it for granted that true life is inward or spiritual life, and that what we are primarily concerned with is motives and principles, rather than rules and actions. This brings us, at once, into a higher region, and locates our scene of action upon a higher platform, it at once relieves our moral life of a heavy burden, and purges our moral atmosphere of an element of obscurity. The question then presents itself with great power and simplicity, "for what do we propose to live and act?" and our answer involves our moral status, and suggests a question of still higher import, "What are we?" It is no longer, "what are we doing?"—that is secondary and subsidiary and is involved necessarily in the other; if we *are* right we needs must *do* right; much less is it the question "what do we appear?" The very entertainment of the other enquiry exhibits the superficiality of this, for we know that we cannot always appear right when we are so, and, on the other hand, we can very often manage to appear right when we are not so.

What I claim for Honor is this, that it compels us to *be*, in order that we may *do*, and forbids us to *seem* and not to *be*.

We know that the nature of our material existence is such, that it answers all the purposes of a mask, that it can be used for concealment and deception quite as readily as for the revelation and exhibition of the truth. If a man has nothing to conceal, if his inner life is pure, his motives right, his intentions just, his conscience clear, he will necessarily act out his real nature, there will be a concurrence between his internal and external life which will result in perfect simplicity and integrity of character, and will at once forbid all duplicity and paltering with deception. This is Honor; not an ambitious struggle for supremacy; not an adroit display of superficial qualities; not a cunning concealment or a bold denial of our deficiencies and shortcomings, much less—very much less—a morbid uneasiness under censure and neglect, and a determination to coerce approval and consideration at every hazzard; but a calm consciousness of imperfection, and a resolute effort at amendment; courage to look at the truth, and patience and fortitude to encounter it.

I said that Honor rejects the idea of penalty; but this by no means implies that it is lawless or involves, in the slightest degree, the spirit of insubordination. On the contrary, its very essence is obedience to law, observed all the more strictly, in that it requires that obedience to be inward and spontaneous, and rejects the idea of external coercion.

The fundamental principle of Honor is a recognition of authority, an innate love of order, so complete and unreserved, that it would blush to be controlled by any power outside of its own voluntary impulse; it finds no fault with such control, when its exercise becomes necessary; it only feels mortified that the necessity should exist.

Honor holds in withering scorn the veil of secrecy; it is enough that the action needs to be concealed—that it cannot be done in the open face of day—that it cannot challenge the observation of all observers—to make it a disgraceful action, and it would no more consent to such an action, than it would ventilate a calumny or perpetrate an assassination. It demands to be able to look every man in the face, and fully recognize all its responsibilities. It thus repudiates every shade of petty malice, and is as incapable of a mean thought as it is of a mean action: if it has an issue with another, it makes it openly, magnanimously, nobly; and it would sooner lose a victory, than gain one by the aid of accidental or adventitious circumstances, circumstances irrespective of the point at issue; it knows that there are victories which are disgraceful, and defeats which are noble, and it never hesitates between the two. It rejects all unfair advantage and will never engage in a controversy where the adverse party is plainly on an unequal footing. We all despise the bully, who takes advantage of his superior physical endowment to abuse and torment a weaker person; we know, instinctively, that he is a coward at heart; but there are other advantages than that of strength, the advantage of numbers, of confederacy, of concealment, of position, of surreptitious knowledge, all of which are equally repudiated by true manhood and true honor.

It is a misfortune that the word Honor, which, in its proper and primary sense, is so expressive of the highest attainment of our race, is used, like so many other words, ambiguously in our language; we use it to express an external tribute as well as an internal state, and, in our loose habit of thinking, we too often confound the two meanings. But Honor, as a subject of serious discussion, can only be taken in its subjective sense, and, when we refer to it in that light, we necessarily view it as involving the possession and culture of all the highest attributes of our nature.

In looking as thoroughly as I am able into this interesting subject, I do not see how it is possible for creatures constituted as we are to cultivate this noble

principle, except with reference to a superhuman tribunal: it is too easy to deceive created intelligences,
intelligences upon the same level with ourselves, to
leave us any hope of attaining the high moral stand
ard involved in a sense of honor, by any submission
to the demands or deference to the opinions of our fellow men. If there is any advantage to be obtained
in this way, it is so entirely relative and accidental as
to make it a very unsafe mode of accomplishing our
object. But the divine mind must be an infallible
standard, and the only real difficulty is in apprehend-
ing it.

Is it then possible, in any satisfactory way, to ascertain the standard of honor in the mind of the
Deity? Here is room for a great deal of subtle discussion, but I do not intend to indulge in it, because,
as my object is practical and not controversial, it will
be accomplished most readily by the simple statement
of a few necessary truths. It is impossible for God
to require anything from his creatures which they are
unable to perform; He does require them to act in
accordance with the principles of honor.

Where then shall they obtain them ?

I answer, from himself.

Undoubtedly, the Creator has ordained a mode of intercourse with his rational creatures, whereby they may possess themselves of his rational decisions, and all that is necessary is to adopt that mode sincerely, in order to secure the requisite knowledge. At all events, this commends itself as so entirely conclusive to my mind, that I instinctively reject any subtler process of excogitation ; and in adopting this course, I find the difficulty met by one of those suggestions whose very simplicity proclaims a divine origin— "only do as you would be done by, and you will find all the requirements of honor amply fulfilled."— We shall, thus, learn to subordinate self to wider and nobler interests, and the question thus intelligently disposed of, our manhood alone is involved in the conduct it demands. If self is permitted to occupy our whole horizon, it will, of course, be impossible for us truly to see or justly to estimate the claims of others; and yet, it is only in so far as we recognize those claims, that we can fill our own place, and perform our own duties honorably, as members of society. If we are not content with any intercourse but that which accords to us an unnatural and unauthorized supremacy, our lives will be a narrow struggle for a vain and selfish object. Duty, alone, can secure to us our appropriate position; no other is desirable; we can fill no other with dignity or self-respect; and if, by unworthy concessions or unreasonable efforts, we attain an unmerited distinction, it must, from the nature of things, be only the precursor of degradation and contempt.

If we can once realize that Honor is, not merely an ascription, but a state, that it is an internal quality, and not a mere appendage, the whole tone of our lives will be modified by the recognition, and ennobled and sanctified by the result, and we shall see, at once, the strange misconception, involved in the idea of asserting our honor, or defending our honor, or vindicating our honor; as if honor was such a bauble, such a superficial and ephemeral possession, as to need defence or vindication at human hands; as if all the charges that could be brought against us, or all the calumnies that could be heaped upon us could change our true being, or make us other than we are.

Our part is to be true and noble and generous and

brave ; to be kind and tender and patient and benevolent; all that depends upon ourselves, and constitutes
our honor ; but for its vindication, there is needed a
stronger arm and a wiser head and a purer mind and
a tenderer heart, and God forbid, that we should ever
come to that condition in which our honor shall depend upon human recognition, or be vindicated by
human prowess. Undoubtedly, we are bound to
cherish our honor; but let it be a living honor inseparable from our existence, unassailable, immortal,
in which we live and move and have our being ; let
us stand upon that honor, but not assume, that we
can vindicate it ; let that honor protect us, but let us
not delude ourselves with the idea that we can defend our honor; it is like that other presumptuous
delusion, which has filled the earth with blood, and
furnished weak and wicked despots an excuse for
forcing upon others the lame conclusions of their own
narrow minds, under the shallow plea, that they are
defending *truth*, when, in reality, it is glory enough
for man to touch the hem of her garment, or catch
one ray of the light of her radiant face.

Like truth and duty and heroism and virtue, that

noble word Honor has been pilfered and appropriated and utilized and degraded, until we have become almost hopelessly entangled in the web of sophistry which self worship has cast around us ; and men have come really to believe that they can perpetrate the most dishonorable acts, and indulge the most dishonorable motives, if , by an appeal to fear, they can silence the voice of the accuser; but Honor can neither be appropriated nor coerced, and he who wishes to secure it must follow the course of nature ; he must sow the seeds in the spring that he may enjoy the harvest, legitimately, in the autumn.

LIBERTY.

The question of Liberty has taken such possession
of the world and will so often be presented to your
minds in your future career, that I desire, before you
are entirely separated from our influence, to say a
few words to you about it; and I will begin by elimina-
tion, because there are so many loose and conflicting
opinions upon the subject, that it will be almost impossible to present it satisfactorily until the way has
been cleared of the obstructions with which ignorance and wilfulness have encumbered it. And first,
I would suggest that Liberty is not an absolute but
a relative possession: no man, no derived existence
can be absolutely free; whether we like it or not, we
are hedged in on all sides by peremptory limitations;
our thoughts, words and actions are all circumscribed
and coerced into a very narrow circle of ordained
possibilities; ordinarily, we confine ourselves so
strictly and unquestioningly within the assigned limits

of our lot, that we are not aware of their existence, and we imagine that we are free, simply because we do not approach the bounds or test the strength of our enclosure, but a moments serious thought dispels the illusion and awakens us to a sense of our actual imprisonment, or, as it is more strongly expressed by another, "our imprisonment within the actual."

It is well that we should come clearly and intelligently to the perception of this truth, because it is by our vain struggles against these ordained limitations, that our lives are marred and our characters degraded; all the vain and childish ambitions, all the silly anxieties about position and popularity, all the fierce and bitter animosities engendered by self-love and self-mistrust, all the pitiful and petitionary existences which degrade our nature and demoralize our intercourse, can be traced eventually to our ignorance of the conditions and limitations of moral existence.

Again, Liberty is not independence, because in that case, it would be a mere ignis-fatuus, a word without meaning and without power. Desperately as men may strive after it, there is no such thing as independence possible in creation; creation is, in one all-important sense, a unit, and its parts are all essential and all inter-dependent. It is a simple philosophical fact, says Carlyle, that casting this pebble from my hand changes the centre of gravity of the universe. Nothing is insignificant. In our feeble, relative views of things, we may undertake to distinguish and may dare to despise, but we pay the penalty for our presumption when the stone of offense is made the head of the corner, when the despised and forgotten worker in the mine brings forth the jewel that dazzles the world.

We may yearn for independence, our pride and our selfishness may drive us to frantic efforts to secure it, we may seek it by all the methods which human subtlety has devised to deceive the law-giver and circumvent the law, but we only succeed in exchanging one form of vassalage for another and perhaps a heavier, because we are creatures and therefore integral parts of creation, and the eye cannot say to the hand, I have no need of thee, nor the head to the feet, I have no need of you, on the contrary, the law of existence seems to involve an opposite principle and the only effect of contempt, is, to compel the Creator to vindicate his despised creation and to give more abundant honor to that part which presumption has ventured to undervalue.

But to return; I said that Liberty is not independence, however habitually it may be identified with it and with all that is supposed to secure it: wealth, for instance, which ministers to ease and purchases homage, which affords to the possessor that superficial advantage in intercourse so gratifying to all our ignoble instincts, and tempts him to deny that fraternal relationship which is the basis of all true nobility, true liberty, and therefore true happiness, in existence.

The man who is dependent for consideration upon the tottering and transitory accessories of wealth may dream that he is independent, but he has only exchanged a rational and ordained dependence upon the voluntary respect and affection of intelligent beings, for a servile and debasing dependence upon all the grosser elements of physical and conventional life; he has shifted the ground of his respectability, from an innate, personal qualification to an adventi-

tious circumstance as feeble as a reed and as fleeting
as a shadow. And so it is with that assumed control
over others which we call power, never remembering
that we cannot possess the smallest real power over
anything which is not already subdued and prostrate.
No relative superiority is worthy of the name of
power, for it can only exist by sufferance and until
the stronger man comes to spoil and dispossess.
Power is absolute, inherent and unchangeable, a positive item in the elements of the universe, a real
energy performing a specific function ; not absorbing
but developing, not controlling but regulating, not
destroying but building up : that retroacting, self-
centreing effort, which passes for power in relative
life, is the source and centre of all our weakness and
all our misery ; it must be so because it is false, and
falsehood is but another name for weakness and misery. The man, who depends upon the exercise and
display of relative power, has already bowed to the
yoke and published his innate weakness and mistrust,
he proclaims to all intelligent minds that he needs
some prop to sustain him in his appointed lot, some
external testimony to assure him that he is entitled

to his place in the universe of God. No man needs such a prop who is not pretending to a false position or basing his claim upon a false foundation : the true man is able to stand in his lot, he knows that lot to be a dependent one, and that it is, in its ultimate issue, "not as idle ore"

> "But iron, dug from central gloom,
> "And heated hot with burning fears,
> "And dipt in baths of hissing tears,
> "And battered by the shocks of doom
> "To shape and use."

And, in full view of these appalling conditions, he resolutely accepts it. Power, coercive power, that power which appeals to fear or interest or ambition, which appeals to anything in man but his higher and better nature, is not divine but satanic, and must share the fate of all satanic influences.

Again, Freedom is not License. We need no elaborate argument to convince us of this. French revolutions and the atrocities of communism have spoken too loudly to the world to leave any thinking man in doubt as to the origin and end of lawless liberty. The dissolution of social ties, the confounding of ranks and orders, the supremacy of the ignorant and the unprincipled, the deification of vice, Moskow retreats and incendiary mobs have pretty well enlightened the world as to the true nature and real object of revolutionary violence. The Neros and the Borglas, the Bourbons and the Tudors are bad enough but they are mild and welcome in comparison with St. Antoine and St. Giles. The tramp of the soldier is an ominous sound, but it is melody itself when compared with the mænad March of Versailles.

What then is Liberty? There has been a vast deal said about it in the world, it has been invoked and eulogized and defined and discussed almost " ad nauseam ;" it has been the theme of the poet and the orator, the Statesman and the philosopher time out of mind; and, in our own day, it is not many years since we were invited annually to listen to the outpourings of patriotic zeal in which the sacred name of Liberty was bandied about with a flippant familiarity which has not been justified by subsequent experience. I do not think we are quite as sure now, as

we were twenty years ago, that America has monop-
lized the Liberty of the world.   I think we are somewhat prepared to acknowledge that Liberty means
something more than the ballot-box and the stump.

What then is Liberty?   The answer involves a
paradox.   Liberty is based upon bondage : in order
that something may be free, something else must be
bound : this grows out of our complex and relative
existence ; the antagonism between our higher and
our lower nature necessitates it ; if we would emanci-
pate the one, we must control the other.   It is only
by viewing our existence in this light that we can
realize the true nature and real dignity of human
Liberty.

The world has been turned upside down, whole
races have been swept out of existence, the most sacred rights have been invaded, all that is pure and
beautiful and lovely and refined in domestic relations
and social intercourse have been trampled under foot,
the fairest scenes of nature and the grandest productions of art have been overwhelmed with ruthless
and indiscriminate barbarity in the frantic pursuit of
what men have chosen to dignify with the name of

Liberty. There is scarcely a more affecting incident in modern history than the plaintive and self-forgetful ejaculation of that queen of women and noblest of patriots, Madame Roland, on her journey to the scaffold. "Oh l Liberty, what crimes are perpetrated in thy name!" And yet what could have been expected when the pure and the high souled consented to ally themselves with demons in the attempt to realize a visionary scheme of philosophic communism? There can be no true Liberty apart from control, and it is a poor exchange to substitute the wild orgies of Anarchy for the feeble and fitful cruelty of legalized tyranny.

Liberty then, (the declaration of independence to the contrary notwithstanding) is not a natural right, an inalienable inheritance.—It must be won and it may be forfeited; it demands qualifications ; no one shall enter the palace and sit at the feast who has not on the wedding garment ; it must begin within—" self-knowledge, self-reverence, self-control, these three alone lead life to Sovereign power." How can he be free to be true whose life is based upon a lie? How can he be free to be just whose fortune is built upon injustice and oppression? How can he be noble who lives by trickery and mystification? How can he be great whose standard is success and whose end is self? How can he fulfil his duty to God or man, who is burdened with the care of his own protection and deafened with the outcries of his own disordered passions? If the demands of our lower nature are supreme, if we must be rich and great and admired and successful, what becomes of honor, virtue, justice and truth when they cross our path and frown upon our success? The man who dare not obey his conscience because it will curtail his income; who is afraid to think out his thoughts because it will narrow his circle of admirers; who shrinks from asserting his individuality because it will mar the level of an arbitrary and meretricious standard, the man, in short, who allows himself to be drawn from the path of duty and of truth by any motive either of fear or desire, has subjected himself to a far more real and degrading bondage than feudal serfdom or African slavery; these forms of coercion have been swept from the earth, but can we lay our hands upon our hearts and say that slavery has departed, when men

allow themselves to be driven like galley slaves under the lash of party proscription and sectarian
anathemas and superstitious tests, when the temple of
Liberty swarms with traffickers, and her most blatant
worshipers are bought and sold?

I have said, there can be no such thing as absolute
Liberty, and, looking at the subject in its most general and abstract form, it seems to resolve itself into
a simple alternative, into what we may call *freedom
of choice ;* and this will appear more distinctly upon
further scrutiny, whether we consider the subject in
a social, civil or religious aspect. In a social point
of view, while, on the one hand, there is no possibility of absolute freedom, there is, on the other, no
power of absolute constraint. Society can only affix a
penalty, and it is left for the individual to choose between his fears on the one side and his satisfaction on
the other ; as far as social influences are concerned,
the wildest excesses of fanaticism can only be controlled indirectly, and the severest penalty that society can inflict is simple exclusion from her ranks ;
if this influence ceases to operate, if the offender rises
above or falls below its reach, he becomes, to that
3

extent, uncontrollably free : what control can society wield over the despot on his throne, the hermit in his cell or the outlaw in his retreat? Yet none of these men are absolutely free, they have merely preferred the pains of isolation to the control of society. Nor is there any more real absoluteness in civil control— the power of the law—the constraint is more obvious and immediate, the penalty more direct and tangible, but it is still a matter of choice to the offender, whether he will undergo it or no, and his civil liberty, however he may boast of it, is contingent upon his compliance with conditions which narrow down his freedom to a very stringent alternative.

The question becomes more complicated when it turns upon what is called religious Liberty, because the range is wider, the experiences deeper and the interests higher than in matters of merely temporal concern ; it becomes necessary to define and distinguish.

If by religious Liberty is meant the right of each man to seek, directly from his Maker, needful information upon the most important of subjects, to judge for himself with regard to all intermediate aid or in-

struction, to accept or reject the opinions of others,
to acknowledge or deny human authority, to recognize or abjure human organizations, to claim for himself the privilege, (as he certainly underlies the responsibility) of choosing what he believes to be right
and rejecting what he believes to be wrong in doctrine, in opinion, in practice, and that his choice be
uninfluenced by coercion whether open or secret,
whether gross or refined, whether physical or mental;
if this be the true definition and the true spirit of religious liberty, then I think we are safe in affirming
that it does not exist and never has existed in the
world ; I think we may go still farther and affirm
that it never can exist in the world constituted as it
is. For, what is the meaning—the fundamental principle—of human existence ? is it not probation ? does
it not imply a trial and a test ? is it not a field of action in which each individual soul is required, is compelled to act out its own nature and to manifest its
own will ?

The limitations which surround us are not arbitrary
and accidental, they are the ordained and unerring
tests of our character, they compel us to choose, and

to choose under difficulties. Liberty is not a negation, an imbecile abstraction, a barren insignificance; it is the ultimate condition of human perfection; it is the result of victory; the battle must be fought; the tyrannies must be faced and vanquished; the scarecrows must be found out and exposed, before our liberty can be anything more than a name, a vain and unmeaning boast. I do not see how it could be possible for us, either to realize for ourselves or manifest to others our rightful allegiance to the only true source of wisdom and of power, if there were no pretenders in the field, if that allegiance were not challenged by specious and life-like simulacra, if our confidence in the integrity of our Maker were not tried by the most severe and searching appeals both to our fears and our hopes, and if our apprehensions of a higher and a nobler existence were not verified by a real and unmistakable experience. It is from first to last, a choice, a choice under difficulties, a choice involving a total surrender of ease and satisfaction, of honors and advancement, of social consideration and personal friendship, a choice involving, if need be, life itself, and which, through all the phases of human existence and the changes and chances of individual experience, has, sooner or later, been compelled to express itself in that memorable ejaculation, "although the fig tree shall not blossom, neither shall fruit be in the vine, the labor of the olive shall fail and the field shall yield no meat, the flocks shall be cut off from the fold and there shall be no herds in the stall, yet will I rejoice in the Lord, I will joy in the God of my salvation."

Nothing short of this can convince a rational intelligence that it is free, nothing short of this can meet the demands of a human soul in search of substantial good. A good which is at the mercy of frail and imperfect existences, a good which depends upon caprice or prejudice or passion, a good which is based upon the shifting sands of popular opinion, so utterly falls short of the necessities of our real life, that the one must perish before we can consent to accept the other; and on the other hand, the good for which we are intended is so far above, not only our reach, but our comprehension, that it involves, logically as well as practically, superhuman energy in its attainment. The good, which comes to beings

constituted as we are without effort and without sacrifice, can only be material and transitory like our lower
selves.

If this is so, then I think we can come to the question with something like suitable preparation, and
we shall perceive at once that the answer must be
contingent; it will depend upon our ultimate aim;
we will measure our freedom by the nature
of our object and the extent of our hindrances.
If the object for which I live is distinction, if I depend for my happiness and self-respect upon homage
or admiration or any relative consideration whatso-
ever, what becomes of my title to liberty while there
remains a single intelligent mind that denies my claim
and withholds his homage? What a mockery of existence must that condition present, which rests upon
the assent of such unreliable and arbitrary natures as
we feel to be within us and know to be around us?
Not only must the price of such a liberty be external
vigilance, but its preservation demands infinite wisdom and boundless power.

All the great minds of the world have recognized
this principle, from Cincinnatus the ploughman to

Vassa the prince : we cannot of course lay bare the secrets of the heart; both of these men may have been ambitious, but they had at least the wisdom to sub-ject their ambition to their judgment, to make their own conditions and hold the reins of government in their own hands; not for one moment would they ac-cept office as a favor; not for one moment would they be petitioners for place and power; they knew that to the conscientious ruler office is a burden far more than it is an honor, that its labors are far beyond its re-wards, and no imposing assumptions or time-honored fallacies could blind them to the miseries of a false posi-tion; they felt, and they nobly exemplified the differ-ence between a tool of a faction and a servant of the public; and the result was power, real power ; they controlled the people whom they served; they did not hesitate to adopt needful policies, however unpop-ular, and their records were honorable to themselves and glorious to their countries; their lives were free; in the assertion of personal individuality, in the main-tenance of legitimate control, in the sympathy and concurrence of the wise and good they were nobly free.

Among the numberless evidences of the political
wisdom of the Roman people, none has struck me
so forcibly as the institution of the dictatorship,
an institution which might, at first sight, seem to be
the very death-knell of Liberty, but which, in the
hands of a brave and free people, became one of its
most efficient buttresses. They knew that, under
ordinary circumstances, things would, in the main,
find their level, that in spite of faction and intrigue
and allowing for occasional exceptions, which are not
without their use in the general plan, worth and virtue would occupy their appropriate place and find
their proper reward, that the temporary supremacy
of the bad is far more in appearance than in reality,
that society can afford to sustain the scum and froth
that gather to the surface in the stillness of the summer calm ; but that in times of difficulty and danger when deep principles are involved and the very
life of the body politic is at stake, the exigency
must be met by a sterner rule, and they felt so secure in their liberty, they knew so well the foundation upon which it was built, its vital connection
with the plan of government, and its real hold upon

the hearts of the people, that they never hesitated to commit it, for a time, to the keeping of one man, when they were assured that in him alone lay the ability to provide " *ne aliquid detrimenti republicæ accideret.*" While there was virtue enough to maintain this institution, Liberty survived ; when the dictator became enamoured of personal power, and was permitted to purchase it by consulting the interests of a dominant party, and to secure it by exterminating proscriptions, Liberty gathered around her the robe which they had defiled, and withdrew her august presence from the sanctuary which they had polluted.

But to return, Liberty has nothing to do with externals, it is a question which is settled once and forever in a man's own breast, and the question decided there is, simply, will he pay the price? To be willing to swim against the current, to be able to choose the right when all influences and all motives and all personal considerations are against us, implies such a grappling with realities, such a mastery over time and sense, that the man who is conscious of this attainment is free for all the practical purposes of human existence, is free to live out his own life and to meet the absolute upon his own terms.

Once more, to revert to the conditions of relative life, they hedge us in on every side and we can enjoy no liberty while subjected to their control; how can we be said to be free, encumbered as we are with the necessities and subject to the laws of a derived existence conditioned from without? There can be no hope for us while we look in that direction, and it is because men do look resolutely and wilfully in that direction that the poet is justified in that inconclusive and bitter monologue in which he embodies the despair of uninspired humanity. "To die! to sleep! and by a sleep to say we end the heart-ache and the thousand natural shocks that flesh is heir to! 'Tis a consummation devoutly to be wished."

The mountain will not come to Mahomet, can Mahomet summon the humility and the courage to go to the mountain?

If I cannot reconcile the unchangeable laws of moral life with my crude notions of justice and right, may I not find an escape from the dilemma, by accepting those laws as a rightful substitute?

If I cannot mould events, may I not more wisely suffer events to mould me? and if all fail here, if justice and right wholly elude my grasp in this phenomenal world, may I not utilize my failure by appealing to another court and transferring my cause to a higher tribunal; and may it not be that the solution of this tremendous problem is to be found in a formula so simple, that he that runs may read, a formula made simple, for the very reason that it has to be read by a traveller who has no time for vain speculations and controverted opinions and questionable dogmas? I may be dissatisfied with my lot, but that lot is, at least, an inevitable fact. I do not see that it will help me to prove, in the clearest manner, injustice against my Maker, but I do see and feel every hour that it will help me to accept that lot from his hands, and turn it to the best account that my delegated powers will permit: I clearly see that I become both logically and actually free the moment that I heartily acquiesce in the arrangement by which I have become a respon-

sible being in a rational world, by which I am em-
powered to select for myself the grandest existence
to which a creature can hope to attain, an arrangement which superadds to the promise of an unmerited gift, the privilege of a co-operative merit. I do
not ask for freedom to rebel, for freedom to upturn
and demolish, for freedom to cultivate my lower
nature and indulge my baser propensities; such a
freedom would only leave me doubly a slave; but I
ask for freedom to choose the highest and the best
that is set before me, and I have it; for freedom to
stand in my own lot and act out my own nature,
and I have it; for freedom to fight (if I must needs
fight) under a banner of my own choice, and a chief
of my own selection, and I have it. By the testimony of all the wise and the good that have gone
before me; by the testimony of a divine life and a
martyr's death; by the testimony of all the truest
instincts and noblest aspirations of my own God-
given spirit, I have it, without a doubt, I have it.

Upon the young men of this generation, there
rests an almost overwhelming responsibility; in order to meet it, you must be free; how can you serve

your country aright if you are hampered by sensual habits, party pledges, personal ambitions? Shake yourselves free, once and forever, from all illegitimate influences, in order that you may dedicate yourselves with manly energy to your divinely appointed task. "Let all the ends you aim at be your Country's, your God's and Truth's." None but true men can be true patriots; patriotism implies self-surrender, "and a life of self-renouncing love, is a life of liberty."

CHIVALRY.

The only real power in the world is Christianity; everything else that passes for such is either an imitation or a substitute, or a positive delusion. Christianity, however, though universal in its application and real in its operation, is exclusive in its practice, exacting in its demands and severe in its discipline, and our frail and time-serving race find it impossible to accept it in its strength and simplicity. Like the ocean which bears the wealth of nations upon its bosom, yet demands from the solitary swimmer long and faithful practice before it will sustain his insignificant weight, Christianity, while it offers a blessing to the race, demands sacrifice from the individual. The claims of Christianity are, however, too strong to be overlooked; it undertakes too much and it has already accomplished too much for the human race, both individually and collectively, to be entirely ignored; the vast majority of civilized men feel that they compromise not merely their safety, but their intelligence, when they openly reject it. It becomes necessary, then, to adopt a system which shall meet the difficulties of the case, which shall satisfy the conscience while it indulges the non-committal policy of man, and consequently we see, from the very beginning, such systems inaugurated, sustained and presented to successive generations as the legitimate development and authorized representatives of Christianity in the world. They have been alike strong in their professions, lax in their principles and intolerant in their practice, at the same time that they have, one and all, adopted some watchword and enforced some special virtue which gave an air of genuineness to their pretensions.

Among these pseudo-Christian systems I have selected one for special notice at present, as well for its intrinsic beauty and its long prevalence as because it is rapidly becoming a thing of the past, and it seems meet, before we consign it to oblivion, to pay a passing tribute to its memory.

The spirit of Chivalry was once a power on the earth, presumptuous, it is true, in that it claimed a higher origin and demanded a more unquestioning submission than was justly its due, but still to a certain extent and within reasonable bounds a real and benignant power.

In so far as it undertook to patronize Christianity and to defend justice and truth, its pretensions were simply absurd; but in so far as it aspired to regulate manners and to establish a high standard of social intercourse, in an age when selfishness and brute force were running riot over the earth, it performed a noble work, and merits unqualified praise. It requires an effort in the present day, when so much has been done to meliorate and discipline human intercourse, to recall and realize the ages when force was the only law and submission the only security; when the rude and untutored wills of semi-barbarous dependents could only be restrained by the still stronger wills of unscrupulous despots; when there was nothing to interpose between power and its victim but the strong arm of superior power; when justice and right, virtue and courage, innocence and purity went down unrecognized before the remorseless oppressor; when there was no safety, no sense of security, no court of appeals, no overawing public opinion ; when might was right, and the act of oppression legalized itself.

It is hard for us now to imagine such a condition of things, but then it was a stern reality, too stern to be long endured. There came at length a revolt in the camp ;. all that was left of high and noble in man's nature rebelled against the supremacy of un-reasoning, inhuman violence, and as there could be at first no available organization, brave and high-minded men went forth single-handed to protect the weak, to shelter the oppressed, to defend the inno-cent, and as brute force was all against them, they instinctively invoked some higher principle, some more subtle element of power to sustain them in their unworldly adventure.

It is easy to see that the alliance men would desire to secure in such an unequal encounter would be, to them at least, a profound reality ; no figment of the imagination, no conjuration of the heat-oppressed brain would answer as a reserved force in the presence of an overwhelming material enemy ; the language of a man who stood undaunted in such a presence

could have been nothing short of certainty; " I am
not following a cunningly devised fable" must have
been the expression of his confidence in the might
which he invoked. The suggestion is forcibly illustrated by the great Scotch romancer in the stirring
scene at Ashby where the wounded champion on
his wearied roadster presents himself in the lists to
encounter the gigantic knight on his powerful war-
horse; he religiously believed in the reality of the
power which inspired him, and that the strength of
that power was made perfect in his weakness.

Such was the spirit of chivalry; such was the internal conviction of every man who, in those days of
gross material life, went forth to encounter evil
according to the light that was in him.

It was not possible for such a spirit as this to retain the gross and brutal manners which would naturally attend the reign of violence. It would be impossible to treat otherwise than kindly and consider-
ately the unfortunate traveller rescued from the
marauder; the tender woman saved from her captors
would necessarily enjoy the respect and attention due
to her weakness and her purity; between the mem-

bers also of the fraternity there would grow up a courtesy and mutual respect which would be the badge of their profession, and the evidence of their relationship, and the fierce marauder himself would be taught by the forbearance of his conqueror a lesson of humanity which would bring a blush to his rough and hardened cheek.

The distinguishing characteristic, I might almost say the vital principle of chivalry, very soon shared the fate of all true original principles in the world ; it was not a failure ; it did not fall short of its professions; but it perished for lack of culture ; it was poisoned by the impure air it was forced to breathe, and while the world looked on in stolid wonder cr sardonic mockery, the well-timed satire of Cervantes gave it the "coup-de-grace" which consigned it to the tomb of epidemic insanities ; when knight-errantry was abolished, chivalry was drained of its life-blood ; it ceased to be an influence and became an institution ; it assumed a body but lost its soul, and, as the untenanted mansion was swept and garnished, worldly and selfish spirits entered in and gave it selfish purpose and malevolent energy.

Then came the reign of knightly associations ; then came the transference of responsibility from the individual to society ; then came the lust of dominion and the worship of power ; then came intrigue and corrupt maxims and Machiavellian policies ; the standard of honor, simple and transparent in the individual breast, became indistinct and wavering as interpreted by the many, and the motto of a magnificent Order became the response of an ambiguou oracle.

The desire for what men call certainty, seems to amount to a passion in the human breast, and by this certainty is meant some established and localized dogma which is accepted as authority and can be referred to as standard in the collision of opinions ; and whatever disguises and intervening fallacies may be assumed, that dogma is always found to be, in the end, the expression of an interested opinion endorsed by numbers ; but such an endorsement will not satisfy a mind in search of truth, or secure the creative purpose in the development of our being ; conscience alone is the ultimate standard of truth and duty—an enlightened conscience, a con-

science regulated and quickened by sincere and
earnest culture is the only oracle which claims a
divine sanction and yields a divine response; and it
is because conscience is what it is that men are so
desperately driven to seek another arbiter. If the
divine spirit does actually dwell in man, its exactions
must necessarily excruciate his nature, and it is not
to be wondered at, therefore, that he should seek to
modify those exactions and bring into a practicable
compass an apparently unattainable standard; brave
and honest thought will enable him to do this without
any compromise either of human freedom or divine
perfection; but brave and honest thought is not
easy to man, and sophistry offers a more acceptable
solution; hence the desire to tamper with the
standard, and when its sanctity has been once invaded there is, of course, no limit to the infringement; and just in proportion to the infringement
will be the mistrust of his position and an anxiety
for external support, which will drive him to intolerance and justify persecution. This is unfortunately
too often the history of human organizations; origi-
nating in the purest motives, seeking only to secure

fraternal coöperation in a benevolent enterprise, the necessary concentration of power involved in organ-·ization offers a tempting bait to human ambition, and the allegiance of the feeble-minded and the thoughtless is adroitly transferred from the benevolent ends to the instituted means, and timid and selfish natures, too weak for faith and too indolent for knowledge, are only too thankful to hang their destiny upon the skirts of an organization. Thus it was with chivalry transmuted into a system. Individuality merged in a corporation; faith circumscribed by the senses; power divorced from reason, and what could remain but a hollow mask awaiting the inevitable exposure of time and dependent for its transient power upon the myopy of the world.

But my object in introducing chivalry to your notice was not to dwell upon its historical development, but to exhibit and analyze its typical meaning, and to notice, for a short time, some of those salient characteristics which connect it, not with history, but with life.

And first, it recognized and proclaimed the origin and true nature of power. The world (and by that

I mean human nature controlled by the senses) has but one idea of power, coercion; ignorant of the true order of the universe, unable to realize the pefect harmony of creation or to measure the orbit of its mechanism, it constructs a microcosm out of materials furnished by the senses, and then seeks to bring all things within the scope of its narrow operation; regarding itself as infallible, it never questions its own decisions, but proceeds in consistent defiance of reason to execute its own decrees; establishing its dogmas upon inductions unsatisfactory to individual minds, it overrides conscience and that freedom which is the only true basis of morality, in order to establish an arbitrary system, which it promulgates as truth; this spirit was exhibited in its grossest form in the middle ages; and the petty tyrannies which it produced and cherished compelled a reaction, which first took the form of knight-errantry in its social, and afterwards of the reformation in its religious aspect.

The fundamental principle of knight-errantry was a denial of the maxim, "might is right;" and the power it acknowledged was spiritual power; and

thus, though exceedingly weakened by worldly associations, its influence was still for good; it was the
entering wedge of civilization; it unmasked the
veiled prophet who had ridden rough-shod over the
world, and gave humanity the hint which subsequent
generations have partially developed. It said to the
awe-struck multitude, " fear not; truth is a power—
the only power in the universe; fear not failure;
fear not defeat; fear not isolation; fear falsehood
and treachery and the spirit of intolerance and the
spirit of coercion; fear not external force, fear internal baseness; fear not hatred from without, fear
presumption within; fear not created might, fear
God the Creator, and fear Him too much to despise
or set at naught any of His creatures; fear Him
too much to limit what He has not limited, or coerce, directly or indirectly, where He has not coerced." It said all this in a somewhat crude and
inconsistent manner, but it spoke in conformity to
the spirit of the age, it adapted itself necessarily to
the coarse, material society in which it was developed, and gave a hint to the out-lying world which,
in one form or other, has modified and influenced it

ever since. It challenged despotism; it questioned
the reality of brute force; it erected another
standard, and proclaimed its allegiance to a nobler
master; it did not actually assert the power of weakness, but it recognized its rights; and while it lacked
the intelligence to seek its protection, it gallantly assumed the duty of defending it; with the blundering
magnanimity of the royal convert of old, when lis-
tening to the pathetic story enacted in Judea nine-
teen hundred years ago, it indignantly exclaimed:
" *Si adessem cum meis Frankis eum defendissem.*"

Again, while it repudiated force it exacted courtesy—courtesy rather as a subjective affection than
an objective duty. The true knight was bound to
be courteous, not so much for the sake of others as
for his own sake; not so much from benevolence as
from self-respect; herein it fell short of Christianity,
it was introspective rather than circumspective;
while professing benevolence and performing beneficent actions, it unhesitatingly put self uppermost,
and made it the pivot of its operations and the
centre of its system. But, though far from perfect,
it still presented itself as a boon to the world; if it

4

could not reach the sublimity of that precept, "resist not evil," it at least took care that it was evil which it did resist; if it could not arm itself with the best weapon, it at least endeavored to turn its weapon against the common enemy : and if it failed to pierce through the subtle disguises of the real foe, it assailed all who wore his livery or were found in his ranks ; resisting wrong even unto blood, it maintained, in the most desperate encounters, its conservative principle of universal courtesy; it stretched out its hand to the fallen foe, and proffered him an honorable friendship upon honorable terms ; it repudiated every shade of vindictiveness, and preferred defeat to victory obtained by treachery or unfair advantage. Would to God that its spirit could be emulated in this Christian land and this era of boasted civilization !

The decadence of chivalry and the change of manners attendant thereupon is, in a great degree, accounted for by the proverbial and unreasoning tendency of human nature to rush into extremes, and to mistake accidental concurrences for orderly associations,—antecedent and consequent for cause and effect. It was quite possible, and it became practically customary, to substitute good manners for good feelings, to veil a black heart and a malevolent purpose under a smiling countenance and a graceful exterior, and, as society could only enforce the latter, they were insensibly accepted as tests of membership; but exposure was inevitable; society would soon discover that something was wrong, and, when the cheat was brought to light, a hasty and inconsiderate repudiation of the evil would sweep away with it the superficial good which it had adopted as a mask; and politeness constrained into the service of hypocrisy was compelled to share its fate, or, still worse, become its scape-goat: for, most unfortunately, while the polish was banished, the hypocrisy remained under another form and a coarser garb. There is no natural alliance,—nothing necessarily in common between malignity and urbanity, nor have coarseness and bluntness any real connection with honesty and sincerity; good things naturally and rationally belong to each other, and when they are separated it is owing, not to any inherent discord, but to the

subtle power of evil mastering the feeble glimmer-
ings of reason in man, and taking advantage of his
myopic vision to deceive him. No one in whose
mind reason predominates can be misled by such
short-sighted sophistry; a good man will cultivate
good manners because they are good, and a true
man will take care that they are the exponents and
not the masks of his genuine feelings and a brave
man will not permit the misconduct of others to
drive him to similar misconduct. He will be gentle
and kind because he feels gently and kindly; he
will be considerate in his intercourse with his fellow-
men because he loves his fellow-men, and he will
treat them with all proper respect because he recognizes, in the humblest and the worst, a spark of that
divinity which, kindled into a flame, will burn forever; coarseness may be better than hypocrisy, but
I see no reason why we should be subjected to the
degrading alternative.

It is Christianity alone that can ensure an unfailing courtesy, because it is she alone that can relieve
a consciously feeble being from the necessity of self-
protection, and thus set him free to recognize the

rights and consult the feelings and minister to the satisfactions of those around him.

It has been well said that bad manners are bad morals, because they indicate a mind hampered by self-indulgence and narrowed by self-considera- tion; they show that the perpetrator has not comprehended the true scope of human ex- istence and the full extent of human responsi- bility; and when charged with his neglect of social duties, they leave him free to ask with indignant surprise, "Am I my brother's keeper?" Christian- ity alone can give an unhesitating reply, and she answers with authority, "Undoubtedly you are your brother's keeper, for it is only in that capacity that you rise above the brute; it is only in so far as you are able to postpone self to others that you give evidence of a higher nature than the tiger or the ox;" in all creation, it is man alone who can intelli- gently and habitually sacrifice himself to his fellow creatures, and therefore it is he alone who shares the divine attributes and partakes of the divine nature. And the courtesy which Christianity de- mands is in accordance with this view; it springs from the relationship of man to man, and is based upon the precept, " do as you would be done by." I know no better illustration of the contrast between the two systems than is found in the poem of " Sir Launfal"—a poem remarkable alike for its pure diction, its elevated tone and its masterly conception.

On his powerful war-horse, clad in brilliant armor, buoyant in youth and flushed with hope, the knight rides forth from the arch of his emblazoned gateway in search of the holy grail ; at the foot of one of the stately pillars lies a beggar, sordid in rags, asking alms for the love of Christ. Loathing the foul and unsightly object the knight throws him in scorn a golden coin, and rides on, in the strength of his stainless name, to fulfil his high behest. That was Chivalry. He traverses the earth, he is soiled with contact and worn with fatigue, exposure and want ; time has subdued the mettle of his steed, rusted his armor, stained his tunic, bent his sword and shorn his crest. That was Life. Bowed down with humiliation, disappointment and loss, he arrives at his own gate, now as ever sternly closed against the unfortunate ; there, as before, lies the beggar, sordid in rags, asking alms for the love of Christ ; but another spirit answers his appeal ; softened by sorrow, humbled by adversity and taught by experience, the knight dismounts, sits by his side, divides with him his last crust, and shares with him his battered cup,

> " And the cup in his hand is the holy grail,"
> " Not what we give, but what we share,"
> *Is proof to the giver that God is there.

True courtesy is self-forgetful ; it calls imagination to its aid, and, with an intelligent mental effort, places itself in the position of the other party, enters into his feelings, and instinctively adapts itself to his condition ; it rejects the motto, " Each man for himself and God for us all," and in its place it substitutes a far nobler and, I am fain to think, more effectual maxim, " Each man for his neighbor, that God may be for each man."

---

*A free rendering—The line in "The Vision of Sir Launfal" reads "For, the gift without the giver is bare."

Ed.

Again, we are indebted to chivalry for suggesting and enforcing a high estimate of honor, and for emphatically distinguishing it from its shadow, reputation, and its pseudonym, ambition. It recognized and maintained an internal standard established upon the highest available principles ; no outward force was permitted to bear upon it ; no pressure of fear or favor ; no motive of policy or prudence ; no regard for reputation or hope of distinction was suffered to invade the sanctuary in the breast where honor was enshrined ; it reigned there supreme, and issued its decrees with an authority which no earthly power was allowed to dispute. But here again it fell short of Christianity ; the standard itself was defective ; it lacked the element of self-protection, and required to be vindicated and defended ; not so Christianity ; her honor is unassailable, unapproachable ; far out of the reach of enemies and defamers, it fears neither violence, nor malignity, nor calumny, nor treachery. It fears not Herod the king, nor Pilate the judge, nor Caiaphas the priest, nor Judas the traitor ; but its presence strikes the accuser dumb, and casts to the ground

the armed assailant ; its silence is stronger than
words, and its words are blows.   Chivalry never con-
ceived such an honor as this ; but it refined and
purified the standard of society; it degraded ruffian-
ism, and established a code under which humanity
could begin to assert its long–lost rights ; unreal
itself, it was the type of a glorious reality, and furnished a glimmer of light when all around was
Cimmerian darkness.

Perhaps the most unworldly form in which chivalry
presents itself to our minds is its systematic adoption of the weaker side.   The tendency of human
nature is so strong to take refuge under the arm
of power and the shelter of combinations, and
such shameless injustice is perpetrated under the
shadow of these imposing alliances, that any influence, however imperfect, which gives even a hint
in the opposite direction, must elevate the race and
give it dignity and purpose.   I do not know a more
melancholy exhibition of human nature, than that
which society constantly presents, of honest and
earnest thought, generous and noble aspiration,
unselfish and benevolent action struck at from the

vague identity of a soulless clique, shorn of its power of usefulness, and compelled to linger out its probationary term in a vain struggle with an evil influence too subtle to be identified and too impalpable to be crushed, while, in all that virtuous throng which surrounds him, not one is found who has enough of manhood in his nature to stand by his side and strike one blow for the victim of calumny; not one lover of truth who is willing to seek her retreat or share her obscurity. Chivalry taught this noble lesson to the world, and it is one of the saddest signs of the times that the only human institution which frowned upon the spirit of cliquedom has become a by-word and a mockery among men. I speak of this tendency not as a matter of regret to the victim, upon whom it exercises a wholly beneficial influence, but as a painful witness against society. As far as the sufferer is concerned it is simply a needful test of his genuineness; no man can rely upon his own sincerity, no man can be sure of his allegiance to truth and his conviction of her ultimate triumph, until his faith has been tested by a relentless alternative; and we

know well enough that there is nothing which presents that alternative with such absolute power to
the spirit of man, as the dread of isolation : to the
lover of truth, therefore, the trial is doubly welcome, inasmuch as it operates both subjectively and
objectively to ensure his fidelity ; but what can we
say for the society which applies the test? What
can we say for the professed lover of truth who
denies to another, under such a fearful menace, that
right of private judgment, that freedom of conscience which he does not hesitate to claim for
himself? What can we say for the man who listens
to the maligner, and accepts his suggestions without
a demur and without an enquiry? To the victim
we can say with emphatic confidence, "Go forward
in God's name, for the test of your integrity is the
power to stand alone."

I have spoken of chivalry in its unworldliness ;
let me conclude by a short reference to its grace-
fulness.

The inspiring power, the sustaining influence of
knighthood was devotion to a mistress ; she was the
fairest and the best; no doubt of her honor, no

question of her beauty, no denial of her supremacy was for a moment to be endured; every victory was gained in her name, and all the laurels cast at her feet; the acknowledgment of her worth was a test of friendship and an affront to her was a challenge to battle. In itself it was a childish conceit which served to adorn an imperfect system and give relief to its harsher features, but it was a powerful and beautiful type of real life, and has been illustrated by the heroes and martyrs of the world, her Alfreds and her *Fredericks, her Fenelons and her Luthers, her Tells and her Washingtons in every page of her sanguinary history.

In one of the beautiful romances of the Baron de la Motte Fouqué he avails himself of the simile, and symbolizes truth as the spiritual mistress of his hero, sublimated in her society and indurated in her service. In every encounter it is her influence that ensures the victory, and in moments of doubt and despondency, it is her presence that sustains

---

*The Elector Frederick of Saxony, the third of the name and called "The Wise."

Ed.

and her voice that directs him; earthly beauty allures him in vain; worldly honors are powerless to tempt him; victory is no triumph without her approval, and defeat at her bidding is more welcome than victory.

It sounds like romance, but it is the grandest reality; it is true life illustrated and epitomized. There is but one principle in human existence which can give it power and permanence, which raises it above the finite and the transient into the infinite and the eternal, which rescues man from the tyranny of his lower nature and makes him divine; it is the spirit of Truth; and to the youth who has become so enamoured with the beauty and so convinced of the power of that spirit as to ask earnestly and sincerely, "how shall I propitiate her? where are her marks and what her credentials?" With the same earnestness and sincerity I reply, "Her marks are within you, and her credentials the convictions of your own mind, for which she has provided one supreme and infallible test, *Do they sustain you ?*"

Undoubtedly the crowning glory of chivalry was

its vindication of woman, and its recognition in her person of the power of weakness. Modern civilization has repudiated the system ; it has denied the honor and rejected the tribute and scorned the worship which began, it was said, in flattery and ended in degradation, which proffered a superficial homage that it might lull its victim into a false security. No doubt individual experiences will warrant the charge ; but such cases are only an abuse of the system; according to the true principle of chivalry woman was recognized as the higher, because the purer nature, and man sought at her shrine the influences which were to elevate and the wisdom which was to guide him ; he bowed before her as a superior being and gloried in prostrating his muscular strength before a spiritual energy which his better nature compelled him to obey. It was the true apotheosis of woman; but alas ! she has found in that sublime elevation too rare an atmosphere for her unsanctified nature. She has chosen to descend and to claim, in the crowded arena of worldly strife and competition, an equality which is not true, and which can only be conceded at the expense of her purity

and her honor ; she claims her rights, but she has
lost sight of those rights in the very act of claiming
them. She has the right to influence and to elevate
her protector, to mould and to educate her progeny,
to give tone and character to society, to be true and
patient and brave and heroic beyond the imagination
of man ; she has the right to work in obscurity and
suffer in silence and achieve in neglect, where the
stronger arm would fail and the stronger heart sink ;
she has the right of unerring intuition, where human
virtue staggers and the masculine intellect is at
fault ; she has the right to scathe the seducer with
one glance of her eye and to nerve the coward with
one word from her lips. No woman need ever complain of her lot. It is not the mother of the Gracchi
or the wife of Lucretius or the niece of Virginius ;
it is not the Pembrokes or the Russells or the Frys
who spread their wrongs before the world and seek
to revolutionize society for false and selfish ends.
If man is false and selfish and tyrannical, woman
has no right to complain ; it was her office to train
him ; she had the control of his plastic years and
his hours of innocence and docility, and if she neg-

lect the trust in the pursuit of low, ambitious and unfeminine self-assertion, she reaps the bitter fruit of her folly when she feels compelled to descend from her high position and grapple with the savage with whom her failure has cursed society. When mothers and sisters cease to be the fountains of honor and truth, and, like the daughters of the leech, cry continually, "give, give," is it strange that men should seek to secure domestic peace by the sacrifice of principles which they have never been taught to revere, but on the contrary have been led to despise? If those whose privilege it is to be sought, themselves become the seekers, is it strange that the unbecoming attitude should be recognized and accepted by the low minded and the vain? Woman may succeed in her inglorious effort; she may place herself on the same level and share the toils and the triumphs of her sturdier mate, but it will be at the expense of all that constitutes her real worth. She must sacrifice for the coveted privilege her native dignity and honor, and cast the crown of her purity to the ground ; she must forego the homage which is her birthright, and the influ—

ence which is her dowry, and the ministry which is her glory, and, from the heights of modesty and refinement, descend by her own act into the depths of a drudgery for which barbarism might blush; she must prefer an arena to a throne and the sword of a gladiator to the sceptre of a Queen. When the salt of the earth has thus lost its savor, what can follow but corruption and death?

" Then the mission of woman is o'er.
　The mission of genius on earth ! to uplift,
　Purify and confirm by its own gracious gift,
　The world, in spite of the world's dull endeavor
　To degrade and drag down and oppose it forever.
　The mission of genius; to watch, and to wait,
　To renew, to redeem and to regenerate.
　The mission of woman on earth ! to give birth
　To the Mercy of Heaven descending to earth.
　The mission of woman ! permitted to bruise
　The head of the serpent and sweetly infuse,
　Through the sorrow and sin of earth's registered curse,
　The blessing which mitigates all; born to nurse,
　And to soothe, and to solace, to help and to heal ;
　And the glory of Heaven on earth to reveal."

SCIENCE AND RELIGION

Mr. Draper of Columbia College, N. Y., the author of many interesting and popular works, by which he has earned a wide-spread reputation both in this country and in Europe, has issued a volume entitled "The conflict between Science and Religion," in which he has noted, in small compass, but with marked effect, a variety of interesting facts bearing upon his subject. While every one at all acquainted with the writings of an author of such general merit and such rare literary attainments will expect much instruction as well as enjoyment from a treatise from his accomplished pen, there is, I think, in store for a thoughtful and observant mind some disappointment in the title by which the book is heralded to the world, and to such a mind the following questions will naturally occur. Is there, can there be, any legitimate conflict between Science and Religion? Do they occupy common ground? are they in the same plane of thought? are not their orbits parallel and therefore incapable of intersection ? are their subjects, their objects and their issues so nearly identical as to permit contrast or oppugnancy between them ?

Science has to do with matter, with the senses, the external, the objective, with what can be known, ascertained, proved ; Religion has to do with spirit, with the internal, the subjective, the intuitive, which cannot be proved, but only believed in reliance upon testimony higher than that of sense, which the mind does not merely receive and adopt, but which it furnishes from its own constitutional resources and secures in its own impregnable citadel, the heart.

What may be Mr. Draper's own religious convictions can only be surmised indirectly and not from any clear, unequivocal expressions on his part, so that it is only left for us to hope that he uses the term Religion in a popular and not a scientific sense, that is to say, that he uses the word, not to express the actual intercourse between the human Soul and its Creator, but only the form under which it becomes known when it ceases to be a reality and has become a simulacrum. Unquestionably what Mr. Draper presents to us as one of the parties to the conflict is not Religion, but Sacerdotalism, or Ecclesiasticism, and it is quite fair and much pleasanter to suppose that he does not intend to identify such widely different forms of thought. It would have been better, however, both for himself and his reader, if he had maintained the distinction as decidedly as Gibbon has done or even Lord Bolingbroke, when he assures his reader that his object in writing his philosophical essays is to rescue the misrepresented and abused religion of Jesus from the hands of its nominal adherents and professors. If that is Mr. Draper's intention we cannot but sympathize with him and wish him God-speed in his undertaking, but we must, at the same time, regret that he has left so much room for doubt and equivocation in his mode of treating the subject.

Religion means the worship of the Creator, Science means the investigation of His creation, and there is no more room for conflict between them than there is between paying due honor to Phidias and the study of the architecture of the Parthenon. No doubt the nightly observation of the heavens brought to the

mind of the young Syrian Shepherd many curious
and interesting questions as to their structure and the
laws of their ceaseless movements, but this scientific
enquiry does not seem to have been at all inconsistent with the religious suggestions which they also
awakened, nor has it chilled or checked the burst of
inexpressible adoration which found vent in the beautiful apostrophe. "When I consider thy heavens, even
the work of thy hands, the moon and the stars which
thou hast ordained, what is man that thou art mind-
ful of him, or the son of man that thou so regardest
him ?" There does not seem to be any rational
ground for that struggle which has been so persistently maintained between the men of science and the
men of faith, and which has met with such a well-
merited rebuke at the hands of one whose comprehensive intellect enabled him to see the merits and desig-
nate the boundary of each field of legitimate enquiry,
and who has pronounced his conclusive verdict in
some such form as this. "If the men of science are
content to regard a manifest creation without the
logical implication of a Creator, I do not see what
right the men of faith have to complain, they surely

are not obliged to think as the men of science do; and if the men of faith are resolved to rest upon the dogma of a lawless and mutable Creator, I do not see what ground the men of science have to object, they surely are not obliged to think as the men of faith do, for neither party has any just claim to the monopoly of error, and each should therefore carefully abstain from forcing his own characteristic nonsense upon the convictions of the other."

Professor Huxley from his scientific standpoint gives utterance to his assumed right of dictation in the following conclusive remark. "Pursue," he says " the nettle and the oak, the midge and the mammoth, the infant and the adult, Shakespeare and Caliban to their common root and you have protoplasm for your pains; beyond this analysis science cannot go, and any metaphysic of existence, consequently, which is not fast tethered to this physical substance, which is not firmly anchored in protoplasm, is an affront to the scientific understanding." And there, according to the Professor, is an end of the matter. No doubt there is an end of the matter as far as the human power of analysis is concerned. But what bearing has that analysis upon spiritual substance, which is not the analyzed matter but the analyzing mind? and what disposition does the acute investigator propose to make of that intelligence to which he addresses his complacent conclusion? When he speaks of the mammoth and the midge, of Shakespeare and Caliban, does he mean the bodies or the minds of those created intelligences? Undoubtedly the investigation which he is discussing will bring up in protoplasm or some other material ultimate, because matter, being finite, has a necessary limit, and we are furnished with faculties which can ascertain that limit, faculties objective to and above the substance under examination; but what power have we above mind which can perform the same office to that unitary, invisible, intangible substance? The only power outside of and above mind is the power which created it, and any knowledge we may be able to obtain of that inscrutable substance must be *revealed* and not excogitated.

It is not surprising, however, that intelligent minds which delight to deal with certainties should be driven by the crude assumptions of ignorance and credulity to despise and ignore opinions incapable of sensible verification, but, while we may be willing to make due allowance for impatience under such provocation, we cannot admire that want of confidence in their own honest opinions which drives men to an unreasonable extreme on the other side. It surely is not in accordance with the highest wisdom, that, because some men of faith are ignorant and foolish, we should allow ourselves to throw away as a useless bauble that trust in a wise and good Creator which lies at the foundation of all wisdom and goodness in his dependent creature. Fools, we are told, rush madly in where angels fear to tread; but because fools are presumptuous, angels need not be skeptical.

It cannot be denied that, as our first acquaintance is with matter and its various combinations, which are in full vigor when spirit has scarcely a conscious existence, we should inevitably, in the beginning of our empirical career, surrender ourselves to the importunate demands and the succulent enticements of the dominant element, looking upon body as the substance and soul as the shadow of our complex existence; but it is hardly consistent with our growing

intelligence to maintain this merely superficial distribution of our component elements, after the mind
has been awakened to its true dignity and its proba-
ble destiny ; when the mind has become capable of
observation and reflection it cannot but recognize the
inevitable dissolution of the one and the instinctive
conviction of the imperishability of the other, and
reason and our awakened intelligence will require us
to act accordingly.

I now propose to set before you, in as succinct a
manner as possible, the characteristic claims on each
side of this warmly contested conflict.

Not being scientific, I cannot hope to exhibit the
claims of science with such clearness and force as
Mr. Draper has done in his noble exposition of her
achievements in every department of human progress;
and in order, therefore, to do full justice to her comparative merits, I will present to you in Mr. Draper's
own words a partial but comprehensive view of the
brilliant array of her triumphs over ignorance and
superstition, whenever she has encountered these
stultifying influences in her onward march to universal secular dominion.

5

After furnishing to his reader a long list of the wonders accomplished by science in the intellectual and economic developments of her power, he proceeds, "and yet how imperfect, how inadequate is the catalogue of facts I have furnished in the foregoing pages. I have said nothing of the spread of instruction by the diffusion of the arts of reading and writing through public schools, and the consequent creation of a reading community, the modes of manufacturing public opinion by newspapers and reviews, the power of journalism, the diffusion of information public and private by the post-office and cheap mails, the individual and social advantages of newspaper advertisements. I have said nothing of the establishment of hospitals, the first exemplar of which was the Invalides of Paris; nothing of the improved prisons, reformatories, penitentiaries, asylums, the treatment of lunatics, paupers, criminals; nothing of the construction of canals, of sanitary engineering or of census reports; nothing of the invention of stereotyping, bleaching by chlorine, the cotton gin, or the marvelous contrivances with which cotton mills are filled—contrivances which have given us cheap clothing, and added to cleanliness, comfort and health ; nothing of the grand advancement of medicine and surgery, or the discoveries in physiology, the cultivation of the fine arts, the improvement of agriculture and rural economy, the introduction of chemical manures and farm machinery. I have not referred to the manufacture of iron and its vast affiliated industries; to those of textile fabrics; to the collections of museums of natural history, antiquities, curiosities. I have said nothing adequate about the railway system or the electric telegraph, nor about the calculus, or lithography, the air-pump or the voltaic battery. I have been so unjust to our own country that I have made no allusion to some of its greatest triumphs: its grand conceptions in natural history; its discoveries in magnetism and electricity; its invention of the beautiful art of photography; its application of spectrum analysis; its improvements and advances in topographical surveying and the correct representation of the surface of the globe; nothing of that gift to women, the sewing machine; nothing of the noble contentions and triumphs of the arts of peace—the industrial exhibitions and world's fairs. What a catalogue have we here; and yet how imperfect! How striking the contrast between this activity and the stagnation of the middle ages!"

So much for science, and what more can her most devoted adherents, her most enthusiastic worshipers demand from those whose lot has fallen under the benign influence of her august and beneficent reign?

But, in order to do justice to her claims, is it necessary to depreciate other influences which have shared her labors and sanctified their results, from the first dawn of human reason to the noontide glory of the nineteenth century. For who can deny that, if science furnished the body, religion supplied the motive and the soul of a large portion of those benevolent enterprises so confidently claimed as the unshared glory of scientific effort in the world? And, because religion has been afflicted with inquisitors and hypocrites, shall we deny the equally patent fact that science has had her charlatans and her quacks?

Let us, then, for a moment, dismiss from our regard the camp-followers of both wings of the grand army of humanity, and see if we can find something better to say of religion than that she is represented by the hangers-on who have stolen her name, usurped her powers and desecrated her altars.

We deny that the Church of Rome, of Constantinople or of Alexandria have the slightest claim to represent religion in the world; we deny that Mohamedanism in the East or sectarianism in the West are anything more than human efforts to dogmatize under difficulties; we deny that religion is to be found either in forms of speech or forms of organization; the binding which the word expresses is not an external profession or an adhesion to any form of definition or of doctrine or of liturgical order; it is an internal union between the soul and its maker; it is a subjective allegiance to a spiritual Lord; it is a spontaneous claim to an indefeasible right; it repudiates all external force either through flattery or fear; it can neither be enticed nor coerced; the moment it yields to either influence its life-blood is exhausted and it ceases to function; all appeals to external influences betray the presence of a worldly or a cloven-footed spirit. The instinct of coercion is, not religion, but sectarianism or priest-craft. Mr. Draper has contrasted his justly reverenced science, not with a reality, but a simulacrum, to which he has, very unfairly, accorded the venerable name of religion, and if I could wield Mr. Draper's pen and possessed his wide information, I would undertake to expose his singular mistake; as it is, in my endeavour to do justice to the party he has misrepresented, I must draw very largely upon the good will and unprejudiced mind of those whom I address.

Let us turn then to the enquiry which is due to the other side of the question. What has religion (not its counterfeit) done for the human race? It has made them acquainted, not with their accessories, their surroundings, their external manifestations, but with themselves, their origin, their status and their destiny, and has assured them, by intuitions stronger and more reliable than any demonstrations by the senses, that they are immortals, partakers of a God-like nature and a divine inheritance, that they are not the slaves of circumstances and the victims of fate, but free-men in the universe of God and masters of themselves, that, however poor they may be in the transient and the perishable, the boundless wealth of an infinite Father awaits their appropriation ; it tells them that all anxiety, all perplexity, all doubt and all fear are the mocking suggestions of diabolic infestations ; that their Creator is their friend, has taken note of their disabilities and provided a remedy for every evil that can possibly assail them ; it has changed for its possessor the whole aspect of existence, and instead of leaving him at the mercy of arbitrariness or accident, instead of assigning him to the fate of Tantalus or Sysiphus or Prometheus or Ixion, it bids him pursue his journey through an ordained wilderness of needful preparation, hand in hand with infinite love and infinite power ; it tells him that the world, his transitory habitation, is not, as it sometimes appears, the devil's world, but a workshop in the universe of God, and that though it swarms with insects which "sting and sing," and produces briars and nettles which torture and impede him, it is vivified by the warm sunshine and tempered by the fragrant breezes and glorified by the invisible presence of his Maker, ever bringing good out of evil, joy out of sorrow, and illuminating despair itself with the never-dying vestal fire of hope.

God is in His world; is not that enough to bless
and sanctify it?   The Creator cannot ignore or for-
sake His creation; creation is the eternal work of
an eternal Being, the perpetual outcome of undying
force, and as even the material elements cannot perish but only change, much more must there await
the undying spirit an eternal evolution of characteristic growth.   God is in His world; not visibly, not
sensibly, but in spirit and in power, and we, His
children, must cheer this night of obscurity—of
trial—with the sound of His voice and the touch of
His hand as they come to us through other appointed media, until the day dawn, and we behold
Him, not by the starlight of faith, but by the sunlight of fruition.

Religion when it is genuine cannot curtail our
enjoyments but only purify and expand them; it
does not vulgarize and degrade what is beautiful and
beatific in nature or in art; it does not condemn
the external world, and its legitimate delights; but
it sanctifies creation and divinizes the universe; it
tells us, that all is good because all is of God, that
evil is only the shadow which emphasizes good to

the relative understanding—the back-ground which throws into needed relief the otherwise overpowering perfection of the divine handiwork, and it anticipates the day when our eyes shall shed the scales which now bedim them—when the shell which now enshrouds us shall be broken, and we shall unfold our wings in the sunshine of eternity. It assures us that our Creator has not sent us into the world to be at the mercy of any arbitrary, self-constituted power—any power which can penetrate into that holy of holies, the human heart, and rule despotically there, which can touch our real being or do more than " beat the *case* of Anaxarcus."

Undoubtedly it is so ordered that our faith in an invincible defender should be tried to its fullest capabilities, that we should pay to the last farthing the value of a possession as boundless as the universe and to be held in fee-simple forever; but it tells us at the same time that the instruments of that trial are not, as we are too apt to suppose, free-agents, but that they are controlled and utilized under the most perfect supervision, for our ultimate good, by the wisdom and the love inherent in creative power; that the true welfare of a rational creature can never be associated with falsehood or treachery or malignity or meanness, that the objects of these degrading impulses are as illusive as they are specious and insinuating, and that it is only he, who, detecting and disregarding their enticements, and enduring to the end the fiery trial which tests his integrity, will find himself at last on the vantage-ground of eternal Truth.

Religion can lay claim to many of the temporal blessings awarded to science as her exclusive endowment, but I have purposely confined myself to spiritual results, for I consider these as far more than a counterbalance to all the comforts and luxuries which science has introduced into the world. For myself, and I verily believe for a goodly array of my fellow travellers on this short journey of life, I can safely declare, that I would not exchange one ray of the light shed upon our path by the gospel of Christ for all the inventions by which science has sought to lighten the burden of existence—a burden often far beyond the reach of any human alleviation. But I gratefully acknowledge that I am not called upon to arbitrate in the matter, for the two influences are in no degree incompatible with each other, in as much as there is nothing in the analysis or the proper use of matter which precludes spiritual affections or which should issue in a result of fatal augury to spiritual hopes and aspirations.

Under the influence of these views, I have almost exclusively confined myself to the bearing of Religion upon the life of the soul—the real life—the life which is immortal because its constituents are immortal; and I believe that this is generally considered its only claim ; but, if we look a little more deeply into the subject, I think we shall find ourselves compelled to modify this opinion. The record which Christendom has concurred to adopt as inspired, assures us that " Godliness hath the promise of the life that now is, as well as that which is to come," and I believe that the record here as elsewhere is correct. I am free to acknowledge, however, that this question, as with all questions presented to rational intelligences, is open to discussion and admits a difference of opinion ; a free choice is the privilege as well as the responsibility of ration-

ality, and, in the exercise of this choice, the man
of the world says, in effect, I have given due attention to the subject and I deliberately choose the good
things of this life, because they are real, tangible
and practicably enjoyable; the vague satisfactions
which you offer to me as a substitute are unreal,
unsubstantial and not guaranteed by experience or
reliable authority; we are in intelligent contact with
this world, and there is no proof of any other. In
pursuance of the same choice the man of faith says,
I too have looked carefully into the question, and I
come to a very different conclusion :—I find by practical experience that the good things of this world
are utterly insufficient to meet the wants of my
higher nature; multiply them as I may there is ever
a want, ever a misgiving; I either need "more worlds
to conquer" or I crave relief from some indefinable
anxiety, and I am tempted by an unappeasable
demand of my nature to drown the one in the mad
orgies of intemperance or the other overtakes me
with the power of dynamite even upon an imperial
throne.

But when I turn to Religion the veil is lifted; Infinity and eternity open their arms to receive me ; the prospect is limitless and the progress endless ; no " pent up Utica," no " shadow feared of men," no unsatisfied desires; Time the remorseless police-man has withdrawn and I linger unconstrained amidst the fruits and flowers of an eternal Paradise.

But, it is replied, all this is very fine rhetoric but where is your proof ? Men and women, the latter especially, from time immemorial have invented myths and written stories to illustrate their crude theories or vent their disappointments and rectify, according to their idiosyncracies, the ways of Providence, dealing with Nemesis and compensation as if they were masters of the situation and could foresee the issues of events of which they can catch but the faintest immediate effects. What is your imagined eternity but just such a fable constructed for just such a purpose ?

I reply, in the first place, it is not a fable furnished by my own brain, but an instinct of my race, an element of the human mind ineradicable and universal; I am not responsible for it ; I have not excogitated it ; I receive it, as I do my other instincts, as neither admitting question nor demand-ing proof; and secondly, it neither admits question nor demands proof, because it is as perfectly adapted to the order of my consciousness as food is to my hunger or exercise to my health.

The satisfactions of the brute are limited to the present moment and therefore he does not demand a future; he finds no use or occasion for a "*spirit-land*," because his imagination does not transcend the bounds of sense; but *we* are spiritual beings, and we must either find a spiritual home or sell our birthright and enjoy our pottage.

If the effort to grasp the higher life appalls or stultifies us, and we fall back upon wealth as the symbol and source of temporal good, we find it in-adequate, uncertain, and loaded with care; but the symbols and concomitants of the higher life are real, permanent and take care of themselves; Truth is and ever must be an eternal possession; Purity is wine distilled from the dregs, in which there remains no element of corruption; Honor is an internal principle unassailable from without; and "Love is indestructible, her holy flame forever burneth, from

Heaven she came, to Heaven returneth." They are all constituents of an eternal existence, incorruptible, inalienable, unassailable, and, though they are reserved, coy and reticent, they can by due devotion be wooed and won and, by an eternal marriage, become bone of our bone and flesh of our flesh; and the soul, nourished by these immortal elements, gradually but surely, itself becomes immortal. The logic of the case is so simple and resistless that men do not attempt directly to confute it, but, as the power of self-deception in man is as limitless as his other faculties, he is able skilfully to distort and circumvent it. For Truth, he can substitute fact or a verbal quibble; for Purity, an unchallenged exterior; for Honor, reputation; and for Love, politeness. But temporary substitutes are not eternal verities, and, while the power of illusion may enable a mortal to totter for a few days on the borders of uncertainty, conscience dogs his footsteps, and sometimes, when least expected, illusion drops her mask and reveals a countenance black with bitter irony.

And thus, while the man of the world revels in success and riots in enjoyment, his success is uncer-

tain and his enjoyment precarious; and *he knows it.*
While, on the other hand, the man of faith, saddled
with Conscience, circumscribed by Truth, constrained by Purity, under a law to Honor and
betrayed by Love, pursues his journey *light of heart,*
because in the home whither he is hastening those
qualifications are in the ascendant and become the
eternal possession of an immortal spirit; *and he too
knows it*; and this knowledge appeases his craving
for the permanent and the real and is a pledge to
him of an endless life.

But not only is the relationship between Science
and Religion misapprehended and misstated in this
unauthorized contrast, but there is a total want of
fairness and of truth in the presentation of the exponents of the religious element in the records of
history. Instead of ambitious ecclesiastics, shameless sensualists, domineering priests, ignorant and
bigoted partisans, hypocrites and fanatics, why not
enumerate as her true representatives such illustri-
ous lights as Moses and Pythagoras, Solon and Ly-
curgus, Socrates and Plato, Epictetus and the Anto-
nines, Huss and Boos, Luther and Erasmus, Fénelon

and Oberlin, Leighton and Chalmers, Robertson and Bushnell? No one will deny to these men their appropriate place in the catalogue of religious lights in the world, and there is not one of them who cherished a feeling or uttered a thought unfriendly to the cultivation of Science or the advance of society in every department of human development.

To select, as the representatives of the religious element in society, men who denied her spirit, rejected her counsels and repudiated her methods in the whole course of their unhallowed careers, is hardly consistent with the impartial attitude claimed by Mr. Draper in the introduction to his brilliant but misleading exposition.

True, he endeavours to account for his course by assuming that, in order to exhibit clearly the antagonism he has so hastily announced, it is necessary to notice exclusively the extremes on either side; but the extreme he presents on the side of Science consists of her most genuine and worthy followers, such noble lights as Archimedes, Euclid, Newton, Herschel and their compeers; while on the side of Religion he offers, not the extreme of her highest and truest devotees, but Cyril, Torquemada and Leo 10th, men in whose composition the religious element seems to have been utterly obscured or (if such a thing were possible) left out altogether. To talk of a conflict between Science and Religion, as represented by Archimedes on one side and Torquemada on the other, is simply to vitiate the argument by the introduction of a new term into the syllogism.

The simple truth of the case seems to be, that, as the divine element in nature has become more and more distinctly recognized, as men have been compelled, by the gradual opening of their understandings and the dispersion of the mists in which ignorance and prejudice had involved them, to see and acknowledge a Creator, they have felt the absurdity as well as blasphemy of undertaking to discuss and determine the qualities of his essential being, and have seen that enquiries into the nature of the Godhead, instead of leading to any more satisfactory or universal approach to that knowledge which is " Life eternal," have resulted in clouding the intellect, embittering the spirit, hardening the heart, and brutalizing the nature of the mistaken zealots who have persisted in seeking for truth, not in a limitless and all-embracing universe, but in the narrow wells of individual opinion—that, while they have contended like mad-men over the nature of " God manifest in the flesh," they have sacrificed to their pride, their vanity and their malignity—to their sectarianism and their idolatry, the holy tempers, the self-sacrificing spirit and the Godlike charity which signalized his claim of being the representative of Deity to suffering humanity—that, while He said " hereby shall men know that ye are My disciples, if ye have love one for another," the chief object of their religious efforts seemed to be to exclude one-another from the roll of that discipleship —to narrow down the universal *sonship* of the race to professional or sectarian dimensions, and to represent the exclusiveness which is the stigma of society, as a cherished element of the divine administration.

The undebauched intellect of men revolted against the arbitrary and self-assumed claims of specialists, who were too myopic in their vision to recognize anything beyond the limits of their narrow horizon; and men of science, outraged by the audacious attempt to stultify the human mind by confining its exercise to a sphere limited by the combined assumptions of ignorance and impudence, and, hastily assuming that religion was accountable for the sins of Bigotry, determined to throw off, altogether and without examination, the claims of a spiritual world, and to acknowledge nothing which could not be verified by an appeal to the senses. But this was only to fall into the opposite error, and to suffer themselves to be driven from a legitimate field of enquiry, because they found it infested with charlatans and hypocrites, and instead of recognizing the different natures of the two pursuits, and applying the same honesty of purpose and diligence of investigation to the higher that they had done to the lower, and assigning to each its own laws and methods of demonstration, they found it easier or more convenient to deny peremptorily all existence but matter and all proof but the presentation of the senses. This method of dealing with the subject is very much like darkening the windows and then denying the existence of the sun. Scientists may obtain temporary relief from obnoxious questionings by such a course, but mankind will continue to ask the questions, and the true and the brave will never be satisfied until they get a distinct and soul-satisfying answer.

But here we are met by the question, is such an answer attainable? Is there, in other words, any standard of Truth in the world? Science, dealing with the material, replies Protoplasm: I see no objection to that answer coming from the source it does. It is perfectly fair and proper to give a material answer to a sensual enquiry : only, the proper term to be used in this case is, not Truth, but fact. Truth is not physical but metaphysical, and to give a metaphysical reply to a physical enquiry is the illogical proceeding which Aristotle condemns, under the charge of "passing over to another kind," or drawing a general conclusion from a particular premise. Science deals with facts, Religion with truths; and when Pilate put his mocking question, he really meant to say, if he had only known it,

" how can we, who are finite beings, give an intelli‑
gible answer to a question which involves the
Infinite." God, alone, can comprehend all that is
included in that universal term, and, therefore, to
Him alone belongs the solution of that tremendous
problem ; and His reply, when it is given, can never
come in a material, but only in a spiritual form,
never to a mind occupied with the external and the
physical, but only to one engaged in an internal and
spiritual investigation. When, therefore, any mind
puts the question honestly and with intention to
the " Father of Spirits," the answer comes directly,
in unshared, undiluted form to that mind, and the
recipient must be content to possess it under that
restriction ; it is His own, sole, exclusive property ;
it is that stone, referred to in the book of Revela‑
tion, upon which there is a new name written, which
no man knows save he that receives it ; it is, and he
should glory in the fact, an open secret between him
and his Maker ; that imagined Truth, which is not
sufficient of itself to its possessor, with which he is
not perfectly satisfied without witness or endorser,
which must be shared and adopted by numbers, in

order to give him assurance of its worth, is the mockery which attracts and deludes the servile tribe of persecutors, fanatics and sectarians. Woe be to us, if, in our search for Truth, we are content with any discovery which needs to be sustained by a buttress resting upon the shifting sands of human opinion ; and it is well worthy of our earnest consideration, whether we can ever pay too high a price for that long-sought, hard-found Ehrenbreitenstein— "Broad stone of Honor "—that " ultima veritas," immovable and immutable forever as the throne itself of the Almighty.

> " In the bitter waves of woe,
>   Beaten and tost about
>   By the sullen winds that blow
>   From the desolate shores of doubt—
>
> When the anchors that Faith had cast
>   Are dragging in the gale,
>   I am quietly holding fast
>   To the things that cannot fail :
>
> I know that right is right,
>   That it is not good to lie ;
>   That Love is better than spite,
>   And a neighbour than a spy ;

I know that Passion needs
The leash of a sober mind ;
I know that generous deeds
Some sure reward will find ;

That the rulers must obey ;
That the givers shall increase ;
That duty lights the way
To the beautiful feet of Peace ;

In the darkest night of the year,
When the stars have all gone out,
That Courage is better than fear,
That Faith is truer than doubt ;

And fierce though the fiends may fight,
And long though the Angels hide,
I know that Truth and Right
Have the universe on their side ;

And that somewhere, beyond the stars,
Is a love that is better than fate ;
When the night unlocks her bars
I shall see Him, and I will wait."

THE PHENOMENAL AND THE REAL.

There is but one light in which it is possible to view, intelligently, the existence in which we now find ourselves, that is, as a preparation for something beyond. Its transitoriness, its imperfection, its imprisonment, its uncertainty and the shortness of its duration, all address our reason so imperatively that we are compelled to abandon it before we can ignore its conclusions :—we must shut our eyes, or close our windows, before we can deny the revelations of sunlight.

But, as it has become the fashion, in many regions of civilization, to turn night into day, to conduct our symposia, whether of business or of pleasure, under the false glare of artificial light, and to waste the healthy oxygen of noon in unnatural and emasculate repose, so, I think, it will be found with those who insist upon treating as a finality, this brief, temporary, incomplete existence; who are willing to

6

accept the embryonic life of the senses, as a full answer to the demand of the spirit for a boundless term of development; to adopt the thought-forms of time and space for the realities of Infinity and Eternity.

What are we? Some inexplicable embodiment of material elements, held together for a brief period by magical art, and to be dissolved and dispersed when the thaumaturgic tension is withdrawn? Are all the rest, mind and heart, feeling and affection, will and choice, faith and hope, love and trust a mere delusion—a mockery—a tantalizing dream wherewith some arbitrary, irresponsible, unapproachable, inexorable agent sees fit to beguile the tedium of his unemployed and purposeless power? Is life, in very deed, a sphinx riddle—a losing game—whose final arbiter is Death?

Thanks to the Power that made me and sent me forth upon the quest after Truth, the search for the holy Grail, I find myself furnished with an answer to this wilful and debasing Pessimism; I find rising up within me, unbidden, unsought, a protest so strong, so clear, that the voice of the fiend dwindles into an inarticulate babble, before its triumphant refrain, "The Lord God omnipotent reigneth," or, in gentler but no less elevated strain, " I know that my Redeemer liveth."

Let us now attempt to analyze this despondent suggestion, under which the human mind endeavors to veil its indolence and its cowardice.

Put into simple language, it merely says, " Things are not as I would have them, the Creator of the world, if there be one, whatever may be His abstract pretentions, is a mere bungler in His attempts at construction. I can see no meaning and no use in suffering ; whatever theories the human mind may construct to account for the existence of Evil, it still remains and ever must remain an unaccountable and stultifying phenomenon in a creation devised by Infinite wisdom, regulated by Infinite love, and executed by Infinite power." And this purely human apprehension is presented to us as the necessary result of the exercise of our rational powers, powers which the Deity himself has furnished to our mental constitution.

And here, let me remark, that there is a wide—

an infinite distinction between Reason and the process of ratiocination, as it is evolved in the human
mind. The former—Reason—the Logos—is God
himself. " In the beginning was Reason (the Logos)
and Reason was *with* God, and Reason *was* God."
The latter is a formal process, correct in construction, but entirely empirical in its elementary parts ;
those parts are Data, and the legitimate deductions
from them : the deductive process can be verified,
but alas for the Data ! they are either utterly want-
ing, or wholly illusory. Before we can correctly
apply the logical formula to the Divine facts, we
must ourselves be in intelligent possession of those
facts :—before we can affirm scientifically, that the
sun revolves around the earth, we must be prepared
to prove, that the earth does not turn upon
its axis.

Now, what finite mind is competent to deal with
this problem of evil ? Evil, as we cognize it, is not an
absolute but a relative idea, but, though a relative
idea, it is a Divine *Creation*, and we are no more
fitted to pronounce upon its nature, its meaning or
its functions, than an insect is fitted to discuss those

characteristics, when applied to St. Peter's at Rome, no, not half as much so.

Observe that rough, uncultivated lot of neglected land; it attracts your notice only by its unsightliness; pass it by a week hence, and you will see, instead of weeds and sand, in one place a confused, disorderly pile of bricks, in another barrels of lime, in another a mass of unhewn timber. Let an Indian, fresh from the forest, be introduced into this collection of crude material, and will he be prepared to credit civilization with any superiority over his cavern in the rocks, or his hovel in the woods ? Can you tempt him away from his wigwam by such a display of order and refinement, as this encumbered lot will afford him? He may listen to your description, and wonder at your rhetoric, but will he not return to his accustomed destitution, thankful to escape from your unmeaning and wholly gratuitous harangue? Precisely so is it with us, in the midst of all our civilization and refinement, until we are able to cognize a higher life than that of the senses ; until the material has begun to confess itself the mere phenomenon that it is, and " the winged and fiery spirit " within us has recognized and asserted its claim to substantial and perpetual existence. As long as we deny the inductions of astronomy, we will continue to believe that the sun rises ; as long as we are deaf to the language of geology, we shall maintain that the Heavens and the Earth were made out of nothing, in six solar days ; as long as we are regardless of the deductions of common sense, we shall be content to assume that the mighty luminaries which surround us were formed to give light to this infinitesimal atom of a peopled earth ; and, in like manner, as long as we are capable of believing that matter is substantial, and that Spirit, which moves, which controls, which shapes and utilizes it, is evanescent, so long, we shall be guilty of the fatuity of living for time and ignoring eternity—necessarily and consistently willing to sacrifice Truth and Purity, Honor and Love to the paltry satisfactions which can be gleaned from the débris of a wasted and abused existence.

What we need, then, is not a more diligent, orderly and profitable use of the senses, not a more serious and vigorous grappling with the political, moral and social difficulties, which mar the perfection and spoil the symmetry of our short apprenticeship, but a clearer apprehension and nobler use of that apprenticeship ; not to treat a joiner's workshop as a well-furnished drawing-room ; not to expect or even desire order, grace and ease, amidst the tools and litter which are involved in their production; not to live as if the school-room were the play-ground or either of them were home :—but, by a strong, manly, scientific use of our faculties and our materials, to put things in their right places, and, by patient continuance in right thinking and well-doing, seek for the glory and the permanence which we so instinctively covet. Just here, I recall an incident which bears pertinently upon our subject. It was at a meeting of literati, gathered for the purpose of general discussion ; and the question under immediate consideration was Principle, its meaning and force :—It was treated in a rather vague and indefinite manner, until it came to a gentleman, who was considered as holding somewhat the position of a patron of literature and learning in society. He expressed himself in substance, as follows :—" Gentlemen, of course we must have Principle ; it would not do to be without Principle in a community ; but there come occasions"—I will not finish the sentence ; the bitterest sarcasm could go no farther in exposing the utter rottenness of merely human profession, the deliberate hardihood with which men look each other in the face, when enunciating and adopting a fallacy which a *child* could detect ; the unfaltering resolution with which clear-headed, intelligent men consent to an equivocation, which is supposed to involve the interests of an individual or a fraternity, sacrificing Character, Individuality, Honor, Manhood and Truth in an utterly futile effort to bolster up a false position, or to silence an upbraiding conscience.* Can it be supposed, can any mind, not already pledged to materialism, really believe, that the idea of a God, of an intelligent originator, conductor, controller of the universe forms any part of such a scheme of existence as this ? That in a real world, a final condition of being, deceit and hypocrisy, lying and stealing, treachery and falsehood can be intended to thrive and prosper, as for a time they seem to do here ? Surely, when men who have adopted such a system, and formed

---

*See Hans Andersen's story of "the King's new clothes."

their characters upon such a model as this, profess to believe in a God, it cannot be the God of the New Testament; it cannot be even the God of the Bramin or the Budhist, of Zoroaster or Confucius, but some demon, from the purlieus of the nether chaos, with a mission of delusion for the ears of those who, believing in lies, have enrolled themselves among the worshipers of the father of lies.

Principle is a word which belongs, alone, to a real world; it involves the idea of stability, of permanence; it has no respect to time or place or circumstance; it is, like its Author, unchangeable, the same yesterday, to-day and forever; it is founded upon a rock—the Rock of Ages—and neither the phantasms of earth, nor the gates of hell can ever prevail against it; the sea and the waves may roar, but it remains immovable; combinations and unholy alliances may storm the walls, but the walls are of adamant, and Infinite power holds the citadel; its strength is to sit still; its method of progress is masterly inactivity; its Divine momentum is resistless energy; and it laughs to scorn the insensate bellowings of Mænadic mobs. If there is a God in the universe, Principle is inscribed upon His banner; if there is a Creator of men, Principle is His eternal motto; if there is a Heavenly Father, Principle ensures and perpetuates His paternity; if there is a Saviour of the world, Principle is the corner-stone of His salvation; if we have two natures, Principle, alone, attests the higher; if we are men and not beasts, it is upon Principle, alone, that our claim can be established; and if we are immortals, it is because the Principle within us cannot die.

Men have felt themselves justified, by their social experience, in drawing a distinction between policy and Principle; like the Roman moralist, they adhere to the *justum* as long as it suits their purposes, but when it fails, or rather, seems to fail, they fall back upon the *utile*; as long as Principle can be perverted to countenance the plans and projects of a narrow and selfish utilitarianism, they will consent to patronize it, but when it frowns, as sooner or later it assuredly will frown, upon selfishness and narrow-mindedness, they cast their scruples to the wind, and adopt a more generous and liberal *Policy*. As long as it is convenient to *be* men, as well as to assume the form and circumstance of manhood, they are willing to combine the two, but when manhood means the exercise of courage, faith, patience and hope, and the endurance of neglect, obscurity, poverty and loss, while they resolve to retain the name, they adroitly change the nature of their title, and manhood then comes to mean success, distinction, wealth and power, and, what is perhaps the most painful aspect in which this human defection presents itself, even those adventurous spirits which have made an effort to realize their convictions regard with a mixture of envy and indignation a success so pitiful, an attainment so degrading, purchased at a price so infinitely beyond their value.

Is it not enough to possess the substance? Must we have the shadow too? Is it not enough to look within, and find there the foreshadowing of Honor, Truth, Purity, Manhood and Love? Must we also enjoy the results? Must we pluck the fruit while the tree is only in blossom? Must we luxuriate in the bowers of autumn while the snows of spring still linger on the hillsides? Manhood indeed! Many an honest school-boy could teach us better, many a pensioner upon the bounty of a university, who studies in his attic and starves upon his commons, with nothing but faith and hope to cheer him in his humiliation and his penury, might look down, from the divine heights of sorrow, upon our aimless and meaningless discontent, with pity, almost with contempt. Shame upon our self-deceptions and our dilettanteism; would it not be better, happier, nobler for us to take up our parable and say, let who will be rich, I will be as poor as honesty requires me to be; let who will be great, I will be as humble as modesty constrains me to be; let who will be distinguished, I will be as obscure as truth compels me to be; I have counted the cost of all this, and I would not give one ray of the light of Truth upon my inner vision for all the ignes-fatui, which emphasize while they reveal the gloom of this nether valley.

Mankind is a gregarious unit; in itself, unchanged and uninspired, it is one undistinguished mass of festering corruption. Hear the arraignment brought against it by one who knew it well, both socially and introspectively.

" Oh man ! thou feeble tenant of an hour,
  Debased by slavery or corrupt by power,
  Who knows thee well, must quit thee with disgust,
  Degraded mass of animated dust;
  Thy love is lust, thy friendship all a cheat,
  Thy smile hypocricy, thy tear deceit;
  By nature vile, ennobled but in name,
  Each kindred brute might bid thee blush for shame."

Hear another voice, from the far-off ages of prophetic inspiration.

"Oh! that I had, in the wilderness, a lodging-place of wayfaring men, that I might leave my people and go from them ; for they be all adulterers, an assembly of treacherous men, and they bend their tongues, like their bows, for lies, and they are not valiant for the Truth upon the earth, but they proceed from evil to evil, and they know not me, saith the Lord. Take ye heed, every one, of his neighbour, and trust not in any brother, for every brother will utterly supplant, and every neighbour will walk with slanders, and they will deceive, every one his neighbour, and will not speak the truth ; they have taught their tongues to speak lies, and weary themselves to commit iniquity."

Descend from the prophet to the preacher, what says the Apostle of the Gentiles?

" And even as they did not like to retain God in their knowledge, God gave them over to a reprobate mind, to do those things which are not convenient ; being filled with all unrighteousness, fornication, wickedness, covetousness, maliciousness ; full of envy, murder, debate, deceit, malignity ; whisperers, back-biters, haters of God, despiteful, proud, boasters, inventors of evil things, disobedient to parents, without understanding, covenant breakers, without natural affection, implacable, unmerciful."

Finally, hear the judgment passed upon his race by a noble and loving spirit of later days.

Fenelon, the St. John of modern times, the man whose heart seemed incapable of any other emotion than Love, gives this advice to his beloved pupil, "Let men be men, that is, weak, vain, inconstant, unjust and assuming. Do not disturb yourself. Inure yourself to what is unreasonable and unjust." Such records as these, coming from the highest types of the race, who at the same time confess themselves to be in the same category, clearly warrant the assertion, that the defect is universal, that the incurable disorder is the inheritance of every child of Adam, and that the only specific lies in those effectual words of the leper, "Lord, if thou wilt, thou canst make me clean."

But while this degraded condition of humanity is universal, the sufferers can be divided into two classes; those who wish to be healed, and those who do not; those who desire to be free, and those who hug their chains; those who invoke the healing power, and those who reject it.

Looking at existence in this light, I can see nothing but justice and love in the awards of our Creator. A rational being, privileged with a choice, and with all the consequences of this choice set fairly before him, furnished also with intelligence to apprehend those consequences, can have, it seems to me, no just cause of complaint against his Maker. His rational powers involve and justify the onus of a choice, and if he find the responsibility too great, and decline the gift; if he feel the onus of the choice too heavy, and forbear to make it; if he rest upon the assumption, that the sacrifices of his

higher and the enticements of his lower nature
present an alternative which he has not the courage to encounter, if he prefer a well-filled trough to
the wings of an eagle, he, surely, should be the last
person to upbraid the generous Power which, while
offering him a choice, has carefully provided that
that choice should be respected. It will be found,
I think, when we come to look down upon human
existence from the heights of divinized intelligence
that there never was, in the internal structure of
the man who has consented to his degradation in
the scale of being, anything distasteful or degrading
in the mode of being he has voluntarily adopted.
The scientist may still exult in protoplasm, as the
ultimatum of his physical researches; the meta-
physician or the theologian may still see no difference between reason and the human faculty of
ratiocination; the sensualist may still regard the
senses, as the only possible inlets of enjoyment, and
the worldling be quite content with the gewgaws
and triumphs of social existence; but, as none of
these things are immortal, the experience of their
votaries must be in accordance with that defect.

But Truth is immortal; Love is immortal; Heaven is immortal; they are immortal because they are divine, and the divine cannot perish, nor can any being, into whom the divine has entered as an integral element of his nature.

I have been careful, I think, not to do injustice to those who reject the experiences of a spiritual life, as visionary or fanatical, because I am unable to analyze and am forbidden to judge them. My controversy is with opinions, not men, with the premises, and not the logic or the logician, and my objections to the conclusion are technical, not personal; as long as we are fellow travellers towards the same inevitable goal, it is perfectly permissible to discuss, in an amicable spirit, what may await us beyond, and I am too conscious of my own incompetence, to attempt to dogmatize to my equally incompetent neighbour, or to criticise his viaticum, his vehicle or his luggage. To my apprehension, matter is not even the skin but simply, as Carlyle expresses it, the clothing of our Me; or according to Gœthe, the garment whereby we see God, and spirit the only rational reality. I see nothing in human life to warrant a serious and life-long struggle, but its bearing upon an eternal state. If there is no such state, though I may not feel at liberty to throw away my life, inasmuch as it may involve other purposes and issues of which I am utterly ignorant, yet it has no charm, no attraction for me; I am willing to endure it, because I cannot divest myself of the belief, that it has been assigned to me by a higher, and, as I cannot but believe, a benevolent power; but if this is all, my part in it shall be only endurance, nothing more; I will not contend for its prizes, because they cannot satisfy me, and they cost more than they are worth; I will not complain of its evils, because according to Antoninus, they are either endurable or consuming, and they do not touch my real being; and I will not cut it short, because, in despite of skepticism, there is something within me which says with resistless power, "wait and see;" and because, after all that impatience may urge, doubt involve, or fear suggest, there is, beneath it all, a settled belief in an infinite Father, who loves his wayward children, and is fully able to take care of them.

For myself, until I am called to something better, it is sufficient that even here, in this embryonic existence, I find within me a power of expanding thought, and around me, engraven upon my prison walls, hieroglyphic prophecies of unbounded development, and I do not consider it an unreasonable demand upon my faith and patience, that I should await, in trustful abandonment, my death-birth into the world of eternal realties.

> "'Tis the sunset of life gives this mystical lore ;
> And coming events cast their shadows before."

Behind me is the Aurora, contending fitfully with the gloom of an Arctic night ; but before me is the crepuscular dawn, announcing the rising of a Sun, that shall never set.

MIRACLE.

The controversy between the material and the spiritual has prevailed, so far as we know, in some shape or other, through all time, and, in their zeal for their opinions, the controversialists have been driven to extremes, unwarranted by either science or revelation. Creation, involving a superhuman condition of being, presents, in its simplest and most tangible form, the question upon which the controversy turns—is there anything above material man? Is there a Creator? And, if so, what is the proof? The usual and most direct answer to this question has been—"Miracles"—"an exhibition of superhuman power necessarily involves a superhuman agent." The question, presented in this form, gives the skeptic an advantage of which he is not slow to avail himself; he denies, at once, that there is any legitimate proof, conformable to the canons of evidence, that such power has ever been exhibited, and I think that an honest examination of those canons will compel us to assent to this position; I do not think that the technical proof of miracles is sufficiently established to warrant us in building upon them the claims of the Christian religion : I do not think I would be justified, either in *foro conscientiæ*, or in *foro intelligentiæ*, in assuming the truth of Christianity upon the ground of its recorded miracles ; not that there can be any rational doubt of the actual performance of the miracles, but that the proof lies in another direction ; not in direct evidence, depending upon personal experience and which alone can convince the skeptic, but in inferences and deductions which, however indirect, are satisfactory to an unprejudiced and rational understanding.

If, then, Miracles are not available, upon what are we to rely for our confidence in a system upon which the hopes of humanity are so vitally based ?

I reply, upon the system itself. The relationship between the religion and the miracles is now reversed; at first, the miracles were needed as a foundation for the religion ; now, we credit the miracles upon the testimony of the religion. Christianity, once, from the very nature of the case, despised, hated and scouted from the world, has assumed the supremacy, and willingly or unwillingly, sincerely or hypocritically, men find themselves compelled to acknowledge its claims.

The person of Christ, the doctrines of Christ, the life of Christ have come down to us through years of searching probation, and, under their influence, we have learned too much to be able, with due regard to our intelligence and our moral sense, to ignore or reject them. Never man spake as this man, was the testimony of reluctant hearers, and the universal acclamation of all subsequent witnesses is, never man lived and acted as this man, and, I think, we may safely add, never man could live or act or speak as this man.

This dictum, however, requires to be presented in a more comprehensive and statistical form, though, after all, its force will depend entirely upon the mental status of those to whom it is addressed; opinion cannot be coerced, and a proposition is valueless when its premises are denied.

Under this reservation then, I maintain, that the life, the teachings and the death of Christ cannot be reconciled with the principles and the conduct of a merely natural man. Human nature is innately and universally selfish ; there may be different degrees of this inherited and universal characteristic, but no simply human being is wholly without it, nor is it possible for any one to cast it off, until he has been raised, by some higher influence, above the ordinary necessities and apprehensions of his race; he is *constitutionally* selfish, and his constitutive elements must be changed, before he can breathe in a higher atmosphere ; it is not a question of degree, but of kind ; a man may profess to be unselfish ; he may strive to be so ; he may even imagine that he is so, but a very little careful self-inspection will convince him, that he has only succeeded in concealing his selfishness from superficial observation, and that when the crucial test is applied, it will reappear with original if not increased malignity. But, in four different naratives of his life, varying in style, manner and matter, there does not appear, directly or indirectly, a single instance in which Jesus Christ acted from any motive of self-consideration.

He declared, from the first, that he came, not to do

his own will; and he never seems to have been driven or enticed from that position. By a slight attention to his personal interests his life might have been made easy and prosperous.; he had but to make himself agreeable to the dominant class among his people, to avoid whatever ran counter to their prejudices and their interests, to fall in with their assumed supremacy and their monopoly of sanctity and virtue, to leave things as he found them, and consent to shut his eyes to the falsities and the perversities to which they had subjected the religion of their great leader, by their traditions and their dogmas, and all would have been well; he would have been recognized as a Rabbi, and honored as a man sent from God; or if his aspirations had taken a different turn, and he had yielded to the common people when they wished to take him by force to make him a king, he might have succeeded as a revolutionist, and been chronicled as a hero, and, as a mere man, he must, in accordance with all human instincts, and in obedience to every impulse of his nature, have taken one or the other of the courses thus suggested. Not only was it impossible for a mere man to have fulfilled the conditions of Christ's exist-

ence, but no human intellect could even have excogitated those conditions, or imagined such a life ; but
his thoughts were not as our thoughts, nor his ways
as our ways, and he selected, not the natural path,
not the path which human instincts would have in-
dicated, but one which led him through opposition
and enmity, through derision and contempt to Geth-
semane and the cross. In this view of the case, it seems
to me to require a far greater fund of credulity to
deny than it does to accept the divinity of Christ.

But this is not all; Christ, while he utterly despised and rejected human distinctions, under every
form, both religious and political, persistently claimed
divine authority. All the demi-gods of earth accepted
complacently enough the honors which were ascribed
to them by their servile adorers ; but the divinity of
a Herod or an Alexander was too brutally betrayed
by their own evil passions and selfish aspirations to
enable society at large to endorse the blasphemous
ascription ; and it is only permitted to remain upon
the records of the race in the form of a self-refuting
blasphemy: but when the calm, dignified, unfaltering
assumption, "I came down from Heaven," proceeds

from the lips of him who spake as never man spake, who ventures to mock or gainsay? A feeble demur, as to the nature and extent of the *manifest divinity*, is uttered by some honest thinkers, puzzled by the apparent anomaly of "God manifest in the flesh," but the doubt extends not to the claimant, but only to the meaning and interpretation of the claim. So far from there being any dignified and well sustained rejection of Christianity, we find one of the boldest and most outspoken revilers of ecclesiastical pretentions, who was withheld by no sensitive scruples from denouncing whatever he considered as unauthorized assumption, while dealing with the Apostles and early propagators of Christianity as with fallible, and oftentimes erring, and sometimes even reprehensible men, never referring to the Founder of the religion but with the utmost reverence and admiration, and asserting, as his motive in writing, a desire to rescue the name and the religion of Christ from the misconceptions and misrepresentations of ignorant and presumptuous partisans.

It was Lord Bolingbroke's intelligence, rather than his heart, that paid this tribute to the man of Galilee;

he was too well practiced in the school of casuistry, not to know, that the position of that immaculate man was unassailable.

I have spoken of the life and the person of Christ; one word with regard to the doctrine, in reference to which it will be sufficient to notice a single passage in his sermon on the mount. "Ye have heard that it was said by them of old time, thou shalt love thy neighbour, and hate thine enemy, but I say unto you, love your enemies." The application of this passage to the present enquiry is simply this, that it implies, in the conduct of those who conform to the requirement, an exercise of spiritual power quite as miraculous and far more significant than any of those material miracles which prove such a rock of offence to the magnates of modern science. I am firmly convinced that any man of fair intelligence and simple honesty, to whom this requirement should be presented, would unhesitatingly reply, "I cannot do it;" and whenever, therefore, any frail mortal finds himself enabled, by the divine presence within him, to obey this command, he is compelled to recognize, and authorized to assume the influence of superhuman energy, working, not indeed a material miracle, but a similar result in a higher sphere of existence.

Such a divine interposition is distinctly assumed by the sacred writer in that remarkable passage, "for scarcely for a righteous man would one die, yet, per-adventure, for a good man some would even dare to die, but God commendeth his love to us, in that, while we were yet sinners, (that is, his enemies) Christ died for the ungodly." Men excuse themselves from obedience to the command by this plea of impossi-bility, but they would soon be convinced of the weakness of the plea, if they could only realize that the same power, which once wrought miracles for the healing of the body, is still present, in a higher form, to renovate and vivify the soul, to enable men to overcome nature by the cultivation and exercise of a more potent and unfailing energy.

Such is the character of Christ, such the impression which his life and his teachings have left upon the world; to go back, then, and criticise those gross ma-terial miracles which, alone, could meet the require-ments of a grossly material age, of a people steeped to the lips in formalism and superficiality, whose only respect for law regarded its external sanction, and who were content, therefore, to circumvent it by any subterfuge which could be reconciled to its letter; for us, at this day, to rest our allegiance to the purest, the highest, the most spiritual system which has ever been presented to the rational man as the guide of his life and the pole-star of his hope, to rest, I say, our belief in this system upon the truth or falsity of records which have fed the polemics of the world for nearly two thousand years, rather than upon a life far more wonderful in its spiritual significance than any mere extention of the scope of material possibility, seems, to a thoughtful mind, little short of trifling with a subject which claims, at the very least, respectful attention and intelligent investigation.

If we must needs apply the same test to the Christianity of the present day which the Jews applied to Christ himself, we should at least adapt our method to the requirements of the age; we should remember that we stand upon a higher plane and necessarily employ a more refined and spiritual criticism: the tests which in those days were *supernatural* are now *super-*

*human.** We do not, now, seek to have water changed to wine, but we desire to see the vain, the frivolous and the selfish converted into the modest, the thoughtful and the considerate: we do not, now, ask to have the scales removed from our organs of sensible vision; modern science can answer that demand; but we are amazed and delighted to find a man who could see no beauty in holiness, no attraction in vir-

---

*NOTE.—"It would be as great a Miracle in grace to see a person full of himself, become in a moment dead to all self-interest and sensibility, as to see the child that went to bed last night, rise in the morning as tall and strong as a man of thirty. God conceals his operation in the course of grace, as well as nature, under an insensible succession of events, and by this means keeps us in the obscurity of faith."— *Fénelon, on the Cross.*

NOTE 2.—Owing to the peculiar depth of the Seneca lake in New York, its waters remain at nearly the same temperature all the year round, so that it is never frozen over in winter and the contact of its comparatively warmer water with the colder atmosphere produces a mist which hangs continually over the region, so that during the whole of the winter I passed there, I saw the sun only for a short part of one day; now just suppose such a state of things to be constant and universal and would not that momentary display of the cloudless sun be considered a miracle by all rational observers?

tue, no worth in honesty, no power in truth, with his
mental vision so restored as to exhibit to astonished
observers a model of nobility and truth : we do not,
at the present day, take a very lively interest in the
legend of Daniel among the lions, but we feel a glow
of cheerful hope for our race, when we witness a man
with the same appetites and passions, the same hopes
and fears with ourselves standing bravely by his conscience and his God at the expense of worldly advantage and social distinction : we do not, now, expect or
hope to have our dead recalled to life by any potent
divination ; He who alone was able to utter that con-
juring word is no longer here to reënact the stupendous scene ; once for all he has withdrawn his material
person from the world ; but he has left behind him a
far more potent and welcome presence ; and many
a loving wife, many a devoted mother can testify that
under the benign influence of that unseen presence,
duly invoked and patiently expected, "this my son,"—
this my husband,—"was dead and is alive again." We
are not much attracted or even surprised, in this day
of scientific thaumaturgy, by the strange spectacle of
a man walking upon the water, but it furnishes an

inestimable encouragement in our struggle with evil, to behold a frail and erring man, passing safe and undismayed over the stormy sea of life, sustained by the same arm that was stretched out to rescue drowning Peter from the waves.

Thomas Carlyle, in his own peculiar style, disposes of the miraculous in few but very conclusive words, which I repeat in substance though not with verbal accuracy.

"It were miraculous" he says, "if I could, at this moment, stretch forth my hand and clutch the sun, but does miracle consist in miles of distance or pounds avoirdupois of weight? does not the real, God-revealing miracle consist in this, that I can stretch forth my hand and clutch anything?" and to follow up and amplify the thought, is not nature with her marvels of telescopic and microscopic revelation, with her clouds and her sunsets, her constellations and her comets, is not man with his science and his mechanics, his inventions and his aspirations, his memories and his prophecies, with his wonder-working hand and his wonder-seeing spirit, is not existence itself enclosing in its three-score years and ten, suggestions of life, death and eternity, is it not all one vast, inexplicable, ever present, all confounding miracle? And can it really come to this, that with the apprehension of all that is around them and within reach of the records that mind has left upon the pages of time, men can ventilate their thoughtlessness in discussions about the reality of miracles and questionings about the mode which the Creator has adopted or may adopt to reveal himself to his rational creature, man?

For my own part, I freely confess, I rarely pass a day without some experience suggestive of a superhuman presence in the ordering of events and the occurrence of unexpected issues and unlooked for deliverances. Yesterday the horizon was black with hopeless despair, the curtains of to-day have rolled up, and lo! the sun shining in his strength. Yesterday a wall of insurmountable difficulty obstructed the path, to-day a portal opens, unseen before, and we pass through light of heart, with scarcely a suggestion of the supernatural occurring to the mind absorbed by material interests and enjoyments. In all our experience of life there is nothing more wonderful than the skill with which the mind is able, if it so desires, to exclude God from his universe, the Creator from his creation. But why? Is there anything gained by the effort? Is a Godless world, a world of accident (terms utterly incompatible), a transient, phenomenal, lawless world a pleasanter object of contemplation, a more desirable place of habitation, than the creation of a just, holy, and wise Creator? Is it better to be a nameless bastard than the child of an infinitely loving Father? and yet that is the condition to which a materializing skepticism labors to consign us.

Reason and logical precision assure us, that where there is order there must be an organizer, that creation implies the control of a Creator, and that his control must be beyond our apprehension, and his acts involve crucial difficulties to our finite and relative understandings; that the orbit of his law must be far outside of our petty horizons, and that when comet-like events occur, they will necessarily produce amazement if not consternation in all who do not view them through the telescopic medium of an enlightened faith.

In fine, the only assent that can reasonably be given to the position of the skeptic involves a denial of its truth.   There is no such thing possible as miracle, in the common acceptation of the word, because, to the observing and reverential mind, all is miracle. It is not possible, to a thoughtful observer of nature, to select any of its phenomena as specially wonderful, because existence in its simplest form, in its most familiar phase, is supremely and awfully wonderful.   Whether it be the sun in the heavens, or a blade of grass upon the earth; whether it be an infant of days, or an old man who has not filled his days ; whether it be our introduction to the mystery of life, or our exit through the portal of death ; whether it be the dreams of the day or the visions of the night ; whether it be the statics or the dynamics of our inexplicable existence, everything within, around and above us presents to the thoughtful mind a problem of wonder which it cannot solve and which can only be accepted by the understanding in the form of a divine paradox.

There is no such thing as miracle because all is miracle.

Law the Remedy for the Evils of Life.

Human Law.

———

What is Law? It is an authoritative command with a sanction annexed; without the sanction it is a rule or a command, but not a Law. As rational beings we are the subjects of two systems of Law, the divine and the human. Divine Law, as coming from a perfect source, is universal, immutable and its sanction inexorable. Human Law, as the expression of an imperfect will, is partial, changeable and its sanction uncertain.

The ministerial profession undertakes to expound and promulgate the Divine Law, and the legal profession is charged with the exposition and enforcement of the human Law.

In both cases the word profession suitably expresses the extent of the obligation assumed, inasmuch as the advantages which are offered come to us through instrumentalities in all cases imperfect, in some, malign. Passing by, for the present, the exponents of the divine Law, we propose now to say a few words about human Laws and their administrators. The Laws by which society is controlled are themselves necessarily imperfect, they originate in imperfect minds and are applied to cases imperfectly understood, and thus, they often increase the evils they were intended to correct; but this defect, great as it really is, is trifling in comparison with the failure involved in the imperfection of the administrators. Our media of communication in this undeveloped existence fail so entirely to express our thoughts and intentions that it is often possible to extract a meaning from our words, the exact opposite of that which they were intended to convey; place such unreliable instruments in the hands of an adroit manipulator, whose supposed interest lies in subverting and distorting them, and it is easy to see how little we can depend upon human Laws administered by human agencies; and history only two sadly illustrates the actual certainty of this rational probability. Living, acting and suffering as we do in such an apparently hopeless chaos of moral ideas, it is not to be wondered at that men should give up the contest, fall into the well-worn ruts of conventional accommodation, and sink at once their own individuality and whatever natural appetency for Truth they may inherit in a timid surrender to an assumed inevitable, and even those, who are in the main sincere, are often content to rest in a position which, though confessedly not the highest, is the only one which they consider attainable by human imperfection. In pursuance of this concession, the attitude adopted by the legal profession seems to an on-looker to be somewhat of this nature. Right and justice are strong in themselves, they are in accordance with divine ordinances, and can lay claim to divine support; they pay due respect to the laws of the State, and, secure under her protection, are comparatively independent of individual support. But the unfortunate wrong-doer, the murderer, the thief, the liar, he is without the pale of human sympathy or divine approval, and, in his desperation, he appeals to us for sympathy and aid. Shall we turn our backs upon a fellow mortal in such an extremity as this? Shall we commit him, without an effort, to the tender mercies of the soulless corporation whose laws he has violated, or suffer him to be hanged unprepared, before the throne of relentless Justice, to meet the doom which awaits him there?

This style of argument, specious as it is, will not bear inspection, it is *ex parte* and *ad captandum*, and it is only necessary to carry it out to its legitimate issues, to present it in its naked deficiency and show the other side of the question, to give it a quietus forever.

Human existence is neither solitary nor gregarious, but social; it is the distinguishing characteristic of man, that he is a social being. But the social element in our existence, though primary and characteristic, is not always predominant; the imperfection of our nature, which continually leaves us at the mercy of our selfish instincts, causes us, under certain circumstances, to disregard our social duties and to prefer the demands of the individual to the just claims of society, and it is this strong and frequently overpowering tendency which constitutes the difficulty of the social problem.

Paley, though erring so strangely in many points of his philosophy, is clear and unanswerable in his distribution of the claims of the community and the individual—of the general and the particular—upon civilized man.

As individuals we need the protection of the Law, but it is only as social individuals that we can secure that protection, and if we weaken the authority of society, if, to suit the interests of an aggressor, we break down the barriers which society has erected for the protection of her constituents, we insensibly sap the foundations of social order, and, sooner or later, will find ourselves in the predicament of the woodsman who, in divesting a tree of its superfluous branches, lops off the bough which supports him in the accomplishment of his object.

But, we are told, the Law is too severe; while it may be necessary for the protection of society and the security of order in general, in this particular case it is manifestly unjust, and it becomes our duty, as benevolent beings, to mitigate its needless severity.

No doubt there are occasions when this is strictly true; but it has no logical bearing upon the question before us; probably there never was a case in which the argument did not seem, to the offender, applicable to his own condition, and sympathizing counsel may soon be brought to adopt the same opinion. But let us analyze the case from the very beginning. A civilized community discovers that a certain crime, say forgery, is becoming very common among them, and much suffering, by innocent persons, is the consequence. Under the influence of this discovery, the Legislature passes an Act, inflicting a severe penalty upon the crime in question; it is placed upon the statute book, and there stands, a warning to the offender, known and read of all men. In defiance of this solemn notice from the community of which he is a member, a needy individual replenishes his empty purse at the expense of a neighbour, who thus finds himself, not only a loser, but perhaps even a defaulter, by the criminal act of another, which he could neither foresee nor provide against. Society has done all that she could do to protect her innocent member from such an outrage; her law, and its penalty, both stand in clear characters upon her statute book, and upon the strength of this authority, the offender is arraigned and required to show cause why he should not suffer the penalty due to his crime. Of course he pleads " Not guilty," and looks around for the most skllful talent available, for his defense ; he is skilfully defended. and sent forth in triumph, to pursue his nefarious practices in the community which he has defied, and his advocate has added another leaf to his laurels in defence of the—innocent ?

What now becomes of your claim and my claim upon society, as our protector from robbery and wrong; she has forbidden us to protect ourselves, and has assumed the solemn duty; what is the result ? Are we simply where we were before, with the insignificant loss of a few vile dollars, or as the sufferer may rather be disposed to consider it, with the sudden and unexpected disappearance of that hard-earned money, wherewith he hoped to live respectably, to support his family, to educate his children and to lay up something for fast approaching age ? Is this all ? It would seem to be bad enough, but it is not by any means all, nor even the worst. By far the worst is that society is degraded, has been set at naught and defied, and has proved herself incompetent to the protection of her children and unworthy of their respect and affection; that civilization has retrograded many degrees in her progress to perfection, and that, except in those cases where men have learned to rest upon something higher and stronger than society, they have been driven to the conviction that truth, purity, and honor have no foothold in the world, and that the only safety lies in a cowardly surrender to organized oppression. A few hundred miscreants once terrorized a mighty city, a few unprincipled plotters can still override a disintegrated and drowsy community. The success in both cases being due, not to the strength of the usurpers, but to the weakness of those who submit to their sway.

But to return to the argument, the Law is too severe. Well then, have it modified ; the same power that enacted it can easily remould it and mitigate its severity. Let the complainant carry his grievance to the law-making power and tell that body of the trials and temptations to which he is subjected by their inconsiderate harshness ; of the presumption of which he must be guilty in opposing his judgment to that of the collected will and wisdom of his fellow-citizens ; of the strain upon his intellect in devising some plausible ground for his defense of criminality : of the sophistries which he must employ ; of the truth which he must conceal, of the falsehood which he must endorse; of the officials which he must corrupt; of the juries which he must pack; and all the paraphernalia of simulated justice which he must organize in order to conceal from public animadversion his defiance of the Law he had sworn to defend. Let him tell that august body, which represents the wisdom and the dignity of the State, and which has been called by the votes of fellow-citizens to the most responsible position which a public servant can occupy, that he craves relief from a position in which he finds his duties and his sympathies so strangely at variance, in which he must either leave an unfortunate fellow-being to the fate which he has wilfully and wickedly brought upon himself, or undergo an ordeal of questionable tortuosity which may be sadly misunderstood by cavilling humanity. If the law-making body see fit to accede to his wishes no harm can possibly follow; the particular law in question will be subjected to a process to which all human productions are necessarily liable, and the great principle of Law itself, by which the universe is sustained, will be preserved in unsullied dignity and divine perfection.

But if, on the other hand, the Legislature takes a different view of the matter and refuses to grant his request, what then ? Which of the horns of his dilemma shall he now select ? Shall he dishonor his State, set at naught her enactments, subject himself to a disgraceful ordeal, let loose a blood-hound upon society, encouraged in crime and strong in impunity, and enable him with brazen effrontery to answer an accuser, " Yes, I have defied your Law, what are you going to do about it ?" Or shall he leave the malefactor to the justice he has outraged and the mercy he has forfeited, to the fate he has wilfully and knowingly invoked upon his own head, and the legitimate consequences of his own deliberate act ? Shall a breach be made and left open in the defences of the sheepfold, and the captured wolf be let loose to enter in and destroy, or shall the breach be closed by the strong arm of the Law, and the safety of the flock be ensured by the destruction of the outlawed marauder ?

Undoubtedly there is an appearance of kindliness and a show of sympathy for the suffering, when a reluctance is manifested to be " extreme in marking what is done amiss," but, in the case of a wilful breaker of the Law, it is a mere show, and will not bear intelligent inspection. It is certainly praiseworthy to indulge a forgiving temper in a case which only affects the private sufferer, though, even in such a case, benevolence should be exercised under the supervision of prudence and justice, and the tender heart be controlled by a sound judgment and strong will; but when crime affects society, when a wrong doer is a public enemy, and has become, by his habits and his principles, a public nuisance, the man who undertakes to shield him, to come between him and the penalty which society has deliberately affixed to his crime, becomes in effect " particeps criminis," and should be held in the light of " an accessory after the act."

When on-lookers see an injured person, under the influence of indignant passion, persisting in undue and brutal revenge, they naturally and justly interpose ; but if a property holder, finding his premises continually invaded, and his goods stolen, set spring guns in his enclosure, and give fair notice of the precaution, no one can justly accuse him of cruelty, or should be permitted to countenance or aid the maimed and detected marauder. Would it be anything but a mockery to say to the plundered sufferer, " You may set spring guns if you like, but you should be careful not to load them ?"

No doubt it is a great temptation to an advocate, who is conscious of unusual ability, to utilize his powers in cases of difficulty, where others would be likely to fail, and, if such a person regard only himself and his own reputation and aggrandizement, he will probably not be deterred, by any other consideration, from a display which will secure to him great personal advantage. But thoughtful men who have come to the conviction that they were not sent into this world to consult merely their own advantage, or to appropriate their endowments without respect to the obligations which constitute them social beings and lift them out of soulless animality, thoughtful men, everywhere and always, have been impelled by an overpowering inward inspiration, to subordinate self to the rights and requirements of Society, and to consecrate their powers by devoting them to the interests of that society to which their highest allegiance, their supreme loyalty is justly due. If

the control of Law is so intolerable, if we find ourselves so hampered and precluded from the free use
of our faculties and the full exercise of our rights
by the barriers which she has erected for the safe-
guard of humanity, then let us no longer tamper
with the question, let us boldly adopt the suggestion
of Rousseau, and fall back upon natural rights and
individual prowess; but if the experience of centuries, the wisdom of sages, the cries of the oppressed,
the instincts of humanity, and the precepts and
examples of divinity all point to *Law* as the only
remedy, yet available, for the evils of our ephemeral existence, then let us adopt it, bravely, honestly, thoroughly, and cling to it manfully until we
find a better.

But the truth is, that the real difficulty does not
lie in that direction. Every intelligent man knows,
and most men will admit, that when a difficulty
arises between an individual and the community,
the former must give way. The interests of the
many must prevail over the interests or rather the
apparent interests of one; most men will admit this
and all good citizens will recognize the force of the

principle, and submit to its requirements; but wrong-doers and their abettors are not willing to ackowledge a rule which interferes with their selfish principles; they regard the State as an oppressive abstraction, as an organized despotism, and consider it perfectly justifiable to obstruct her processes and defy her authority whenever concealment or fraud or perjury will enable them to do so with impunity. Short sighted as this policy is, it is perfectly consistent with the intellectual status of the victims of selfishness, of that narrowness of mind which prefers adroitness to simplicity, cunning to wisdom, success to justice, fraud to veracity, the individual to the community, the temporal to the eternal.

I recollect being present at a colloquy between two acquaintances, in which one of the parties remonstrated against a method, proposed by the other, to secure certain pecuniary advantages. "Don't talk to me," was the reply, " of your hampering, old womanish principles; I go in for success." "So do I," said the other, " but what do you call success? Is it ten thousand dollars, or one hundred thousand, or a million? If that is your standard, of course

8

there is nothing more to be said upon the subject ; human logic may change an opinion, but it cannot elevate a standard ; but, if that million is to be purchased at the expense of one atom of truth, of the most trifling infringement of the rights of the neighbour, of the demands of honor, or the warnings of conscience, I would rather sink the whole in the depths of the sea than soil my fingers with the touch of a single coin."

And does it require any great effort of mind, any power of imagination, any depth of philosophy to convince a rational intelligence that there is no other view of human life and human morality at all consistent with wisdom and true manhood ? Can it be necessary to prove to a thinking being, that he has two natures, and that the difference in their value is infinite, that matter perishes, and that spirit is immortal, that silver and gold are corruptible, unsatisfying, burdensome, and that thought and its constituents, truth, purity, justice, honor and love are, in their very nature, indestructible ? No! wherever there is *mind* it inevitably recognizes and enforces the distinction ; but *mind* is a gift and, like all other gifts, it must be estimated, exercised and cultivated or it will either perish in inanity or smoul-- der in the ashes of a sophisticated intelligence ; and it is sad to see how, by the neglect of this precau- tion, men may walk about on God's earth veritable ghosts, literal appearances, out of which the sub- stantial element has long since departed, leaving only a few dying embers to eke out the last gasps of a fatuous existence. *Turpis universo non congruens.*

Gouverneur Morris, in his diary in Paris during the revolution, records an interview with Mirabeau, and, while testifying to his great natural powers con- cludes his estimate with these emphatic words, " His understanding is, I fear, impaired by the perversion of his heart," and in conversation with a distinguished member of our own bar, now no more, I was both surprised and gratified by an apothegm the legiti- mate converse of the same impressive thought, " The pursuit of truth," he said, " enlarges the intellect." If this be true, as cannot be doubted, what must neces- sarily be the condition of a mind habitually em- ployed in the service of sophistry? Habitually subordi- nating truth, justice and honor to the factitious claims

of absorbing individuality or overawing cliquedom?
And with regard to this last, it may be specially remarked that, while individual audacity can be met
and mastered by individual prowess, it requires superhuman power to encounter successfully a combined attack, and it is well for those who have preferred their manhood to the protection of a clique—
who decline to sink their individuality in the emas-
culating ease afforded by unconditional pledges of
support, that they have in reserve an unseen power,
which holds in check unrighteous combinations, and
laughs to scorn the cunning of their petty devices.

I would take this occasion to urge upon the consideration of young men, not yet enthralled in the
net of partisanship, and whose minds are still fragrant with the aroma of divine simplicity, whether
any earthly object can possibly repay them for the
loss of that self-respect and self-possession, which
conscious integrity alone can afford, and the testimony of conscience alone ensure. Will it be nothing, think you, to be enabled to stand alone, amidst
the ruin of fortune, the desertion of friends, the
contempt of the prosperous, the plottings of the

wily, the slanders of the unscrupulous, and the triumph of the unfriendly, in unshaken reliance upon the invincibility of Truth, and the immortality of her votaries? Can you be insensible to the un utterable satisfaction of the standard-bearer who comes out of the fight disfigured by his scars, but with his banner aloft? Will external pomp repay you for internal power? Will wealth, will reputation suffice you when honesty repudiates the one and truth the other?

I will not quote Socrates, I will not refer to a greater than Socrates. I will leave you to the whispers of your better self, I will commend you to the warnings of conscience and the voice of God.

LAW THE REMEDY FOR THE EVILS OF LIFE.

DIVINE LAW.

An intelligent perception of the imperfection of our nature is not a pleasant experience. That we have in ourselves, no germ of virtue which can be cultivated, by due personal effort, into a perfect outgrowth, is a conviction not very flattering to our pride of selfhood; nevertheless, all the intelligence and all the honesty of the human mind, whenever and wherever they have been permitted to develop themselves, have compelled it to make the humiliating confession; humiliating, because, whatever may be the relative intellectual power of the thinker, that power must be attended by the simplicity of childhood, before it can be of any real avail in the pursuit of Truth; and it is in this, as in many other departments of human life, that the justice and the impartiality of the divine arrangements are clearly exhibited. A slow but modest and teachable understanding will come sooner and more thoroughly to the perception of Truth than a brilliant intellect staggering under the consciousness of relative superiority : felicitous diction and faultless logic have tempted many an aspiring genius into regions of thought, where the splendor of the dress served, only more perfectly, to conceal the skeleton beneath.

We naturally view ourselves as relative beings, and it is necessary that we should do so in order to fulfil our relative duties ; but we have an absolute status as well, and it is from this point that we must take note of our characters, if we wish to elevate them in the scale of being; we must weigh ourselves, not against imperfect humanity, but against perfect divinity, if we wish to learn in order that we may modify our relationship to the divine.

I confess that I am appalled in the presence of this necessity. It is easy enough to convince myself that I am better than this robber or that murderer, this liar or that swindler, though even here I may be mistaken, when opportunities and standards and hidden motives are taken into consideration. But when I compare my best graces, my highest virtues, my purest motives with the holiness and the purity, the forbearance and the love which even I can attach to the all-perfect Creator, I do not find in myself much room for gratulation, even if I can resist the impulse to lay my mouth in the dust and cry *"unclean."*

Now, what am I to do with this over-powering sense of ill-desert? Am I, even in a worldly point of view, willing to be the selfish, low-motived, narrow-minded creature that, in the depths of my conscience, I find myself to be? A reptile crawling upon the face of God's beautiful world—a discord in creation—*"turpis universo non congruens?"* Or, finding that I cannot change the absolute fact, shall I take refuge—to use a military term—in a change of base, and content myself with a relative view of my condition which superficially—and only superficially—gives me a vague hope that I may possibly be not quite so low in the scale of being as some of my unfortunate fellow victims, or, as Dr. Paley quaintly expresses it, just on the safe side of the very narrow line which separates the lowest man in Heaven from the highest in Hell? Verily, if it comes to this, I feel that I would have a just right to decline altogether an existence imposed upon my feebleness by an arbitrary, irrational and utterly selfish power.

But must it come to this ? Is there no accredited way in which the question may be so encountered, as to escape from a pessimism so revolting to all the best instincts of my being? Throughout recorded history, the highest types of the race, with one consent, insist that they have found one ; and, for my own part, I feel myself rationally compelled to adopt the view which, not only represents my own honest conviction, but comes to me endorsed by the noblest intellects and the purest spirits which have signalized and adorned humanity.

The spirit of God, necessarily in contact with his rational creation, under the guise of reason and conscience, has given from the earliest recorded times, through the medium of inspiration, an authoritative assurance of his presence within us, and we see, in consequence, the mind of man historically developed through successive dispensations of gradually increasing brilliancy, until, in these latter days, the Revelation of Jesus Christ has perfected the system, by the announcement of a divine humanity, and thus "brought Life and Immortality to light." I say, *has perfected the system*, because I believe that a diligent and honest examination of his record will convince any unprejudiced mind that in that announcement, all that could be done by the Creator, consistently with his supreme gift of rationality, has been done to enable a free spirit to attain the true end of his creation.

The Christian Revelation, coming to us, as it does, under the prepossessing title of a gospel, addresses us in perfectly honest simplicity ; it does not seek to attract our regard by any undue effort at conciliation; it tells us plainly that we were "born in sin," thus indirectly assuring us of course, that we are not responsible for this apparently unfortunate introduction into our present existence, it simply states the fact without seeking to gratify our pride of intellect by any metaphysical explanation of its rationale ; it is enough that God has so ordained it. Even Paul, in his trained and masterful encounter with the Gentile and the Jew—the Roman and the Hebrew—while he fearlessly expounds all that has been revealed, never attempts to go behind the scenes, to account for

Revelation, or to reconcile the Acts of the Creator with the wisdom of the creature. " Nay, but Oh, man," he expostulates with the objector, " who art thou that repliest against God? Shall the thing formed say to him that formed it, why hast thou made me thus ?"

It has been reserved for the growing intelligence of the race, vivified by the sunlight of centuries, to perceive that the whole system of rational existence, which raises man above the rest of creation, and makes him divine, would be overturned if any attempt to secure his reception of truth by outside interference were to put a slight upon his crowning glory, the freedom of his will.

But this by the way. The point which now concerns us is *the remedy*, and, as our own consent and co-operation are involved in its successful application, this remedy is presented in a form, legible by a child, and yet, challenging the scrutiny of the manliest intellect.

Let us address ourselves in good faith to the investigation which it invites.

We were " born in sin," and for this involuntary

evil we are of course wholly irresponsible, and we
need not therefore seek to avoid the blame by imposing it upon some mythical *first man* who "brought
death into the world, and all our woe;" the maker of
the world is quite able to bear upon his own shoulders the consequences of all his creative acts, and we
need not feel called upon to put any strain upon our
finite understandings, by taxing our ingenuity to account for those acts.

But if there is any mode presented to us, by which
we can meet the evil and rid ourselves of an incubus,
which presses so heavily upon us, dogging our footsteps and embittering our existence, then, undoubtedly, we are responsible for all that we suffer by re-
maining wilful victims of its deadly blight. And
here it is that the gospel of Christ comes to the rescue, with absolute accuracy and plenary power; and
it does this as before remarked, with uncompromising sincerity and confidence in the power of truth.
It tells the patient plainly, you cannot cure yourself, it is a spiritual disease whose diagnosis you
cannot compass; you did not create yourself, and the
workings of that wonderful machine whose compli-

cations are involved in your existence, are far more beyond your comprehension than a steam engine is beyond the comprehension of an infant of days.

You cannot cure yourself, but, by the same token, your Creator can ; he who formed the instrument can reform it at his will, and his benevolence is as inexhaustible as his power. If it was worth his while to create you at all, it surely is worth his while to sustain and perfect his creation, and to fulfil the promise of immortality implied in the gift of immortal instincts and premonitions.

But, though the remedy which the Creator has offered for our congenital disease is given freely and with all the generosity and self-sacrifice of a loving parent, it is not given unconditionally ; though the condition still respects our rationality, it is not imposed arbitrarily or to vindicate a creative right, but from the necessity of the case and entirely in the interest of the beneficiary, in order that his vital characteristic—his freedom of choice—should not be overridden, his rationality disregarded and he become an unconscious, involuntary reflector of the divine Omnipotence. The condition, therefore, which is necessary to vindicate his manhood and to indicate his free will in the premises, is that he manifest, by some unequivocal act, his *desire* for the remedy, and as the universal expression of desire is *asking*, he is told to "ask and it shall be given."

Thus far the case is perfectly simple, the transaction, momentous as it is, is encumbered by no side-issues, but is presented in a form plain enough for the comprehension of the feeblest understanding. The main point—the patient's desire for cure—being thus secured, there is room now for all the satisfactions which may facilitate or alleviate the progress of the work ; information may be given, explanations conceded, and natural curiosity indulged, as to the mode of the interposition. What shall I ask for? is the question which now presents itself to the mind of the enquirer, and the answer comes with all the clearness and directness which the occasion demands. Remember now, it suggests, that you have dismissed sense and all its interests from your regard, and have set your feet upon higher ground ; you need no longer concern yourself about your material necessities, they are all involved, with unerring accuracy, in the one single object which is set before you as the sum and substance of your present requirements; having passed safely over the first stage of your journey in search of the truth, the question which now arises is, as has been already suggested, what shall you ask for? Your wants are legion, you are an embodied destitution; as your creator is inexhaustible fullness, so are you bottomless emptiness. Can such emptiness ever be filled? Can such destitution ever be satisfied? "Open thy mouth wide" says the word of inspiration, "Open thy mouth wide and I will fill it;" and if your reason demands a more specific answer to a question, in itself so broad and comprehensive, address yourself once more to the source of inspired wisdom, and you will there find a ready rejoinder awaiting your demand, for you will be met by such a clear, intelligent and altogether sufficient answer as is contained in the very words themselves of the divine man to whom we look as the author and founder of the faith which is now the standard of the advanced guard of humanity. "If ye being evil," he said to the throng of hungering intelligences around him, "If ye being evil, know how to give good gifts to your children, how much more shall your Father in heaven give the *holy spirit* to them that *ask*;" and if your still unsatisfied reason requires a farther insight into the mode of so mysterious an operation, you are not left to the cold comfort of a dry submissive faith, but you are frankly and authoritatively assured that that spirit, that very spirit which you are thus urged to invoke, shall guide you into *all truth;* and finally, as the ordained issue of this orderly and systematic evolution, this truth shall make you *free indeed*, free of the universe, not mere jail delivery, not a relaxation of your bondage to time and sense, not a withdrawal of the limitations of material existence, not merely passive freedom—the freedom of the will—but now at length as your complete emancipation from all the restraints of a created nature, *Free agency*; because, being now in entire accord with the will which controls the universe, you can safely be trusted to *act* as well as to will under the promptings of a divine initiative. It is perfectly true that in this stage of your existence you are nothing but an organized form of destitution; but you are in very serious error as to the nature and

seat of that destitution ; you imagine that it is merely
a defect of your temporal existence—of your sensual
nature ; but, if you will think a moment, you will
easily perceive that you are mistaken in this view of
your condition. The actual wants of the body are
very few and easily supplied; taking the world at
large, its production far exceeds the wants of its in-
habitants ; only equalize the distribution, and bring
human desire within rational limits, and there would
not be a destitute mortal on the face of the globe.
The poverty which disgraces humanity is not charge-
able upon nature, but upon man; not upon what he
is unable to produce, but upon what he is able
and determined to appropriate, and thus clearly
not upon our physical organization, but upon
our spiritual nurture and its legitimate results, and it
is in that direction that we must look for the origin
and seat of our hopeless disorder. Our true poverty
is not material but spiritual, it is rooted in that gnaw-
ing worm of avarice—that " *sacra fames auri*," which
an intelligent pagan abjured—that "vile yellow slave"
which an Indian nabob anathematized, which stimu-
lates our appetite for gain, whether it be of money

or of fame, of pleasure or of power, and indicates an utter want of confidence in the truth and the love of our Maker, and proves that the *faith* which we profess is not *confiding trust, but inoperative belief.* It is a disease utterly incurable by any human specific, and which will only yield to the *transforming* influence of the Spirit of God, enlarging the mental vision to the scope of a boundless horizon, and anticipating the judgment of that decisive hour when Time and Eternity shall stand at our bar and await our decision.

Let this point be fairly settled and we are at once essentially free. The Spirit of God, dwelling within a man and animating his existence, precludes the possibility of restraint: the only rational ground for any curtailment lies in the interest of our eternal state, and, as that is secured by a radical change in our motives and aims, no reasonable indulgence need be denied us; our desires being subordinated to our immortal interests may now be safely and generously gratified.

In the face of such an unanswerable demonstration as this, taken word for word from our sacred records—those records which we ourselves profess to consider sacred—how is it that intelligent beings can be content to remain in ignorance or indifference upon the only subject which is of any real importance to minds capable of immortal apprehensions? How is it that we can not only undergo, so blindly and stupidly, our daily and hourly experiences, as to deny the possibility of miraculous interference in the on-going of material existence, when the universe of matter is nothing but one stupendous, inexplicable miracle; but, by the same wonderful power of self-stultification, can resolutely shut our eyes to the far more impressive display of superhuman activity in a revelation bearing, in its perfect adaptation to our spiritual demands, the impress of an all-embracing divinity.

And, in this connection, permit me to remark as an "*obiter dictum,*" of how little avail human reasoning—persuasive endeavor—has ever been found in matters of spiritual import. How can this be accounted for, except upon the concession, that there is a divinity astir within us? We yield to human demonstration when it is applied to matters which concern the body, the external, the

material, because relative considerations are here
properly in place, and we are compelled to
acknowledge the power of an intellect which is manifestly superior to our own ; but, when the investigation involves a spiritual experience, we are consciously upon higher ground—in a superhuman atmosphere—and we instinctively reject all lower
influences.   When the divine is called into requisi-
tion, created intelligences, differ as they may among
themselves, sink into one dead level of impotence
and insignificance, and, in an enquiry of this nature,
we need, not candle-light, nor gas-light, nor even
electric-light, but *sunlight.*

What every rational being proposes to himself is
his ultimate and unchangeable welfare ; or in other
words, as we cannot help feeling ourselves, in this
stage of our development, in a region of " change
and decay," we irresistibly yearn for stability and
perpetuity; or, to express the thought metaphorically, we are travellers in a howling desert, and, we
long for the permanence and security of *home.*

But our ability to proceed on our journey to this
home varies indefinitely.   Our personal vigor, our

means of locomotion, our strength of will, the force of temptation and a thousand undefinable consider- ations (still speaking metaphorically) concur to re- lease the originator of our being from any possible charge of injustice in the distribution of his gifts, inasmuch as the ultimate need of each individual, that is, his ability to reach his journey's end, which is the only proper object of his solicitude, is made to rest, not upon any question of gifts and graces, but solely upon the use made of them by the recipient. Not the possessor of ten talents, but he who has used his talents, whether ten or one, most faithfully—most in accordance with the will and wisdom of the giver—will be found highest in the scale of being, in that world of reality, whither we are all so rapidly hastening.

It has been my lot to converse with men of very varying powers of mind upon the subject of our human existence, and the result of these colloquies— the impression they have made upon my mind—is distinctly this, that I have found more satisfactory views, clearer light, more unencumbered receptivity, freer thought, simpler and more lucid apprehensions of all the deeper questions of spiritual import, that is, of infinite and absolute being, in minds of unpretending, self-respecting, truth-loving intelligence, than in minds encumbered with the conviction of their own relative profundity—in minds whose satisfaction lay in teaching rather than in learning, in dogmatizing rather than in seeking truth, in uttering themselves rather than in unfolding revelation. The finest intellect, by far, that I have encountered in my literary explorations, has given to the world an unequalled exposition of the relationship between man and his Maker, and yet the whole of that vast subject is contained, as in a vital germ of infinite expansion, in one simple utterance of divine inspiration. "In him we live and move and have our being."

But what of all this unsatisfying fruit of human speculation? Is there anything strange or paradoxical in the conviction, that such a creation as man will not be left in the imperfect condition in which we find him in this prenatal term of his existence? That an embryo of such limitless promise is assuredly intended to come to the birth? That the acorn will, necessarily, expand into the oak? That the shell must, eventually, yield to the pressure of organized vitality, which it encloses? If this be credulity, let us proudly and joyfully respond to a charge so agreeable to our reason and all our diviner instincts.

In a symposium of learned doctors, held some years ago, at which the subject of a future life was under discussion, I remember that one of those who took part in the debate contended that the only life which remains for man beyond the grave is the unconscious aroma of his temporal existence—his transitory and evaporating contribution to the sum of being. Men have a right to their opinions, and we are subject to just censure, when we treat them with disrespect, but opinions are not accidental, they are the legitimate result of antecedent habits of mind, and when the previous life of a rational intelligence inclines him to deny posthumous exist-ence, it would not seem an unfair conclusion, that he mistrusts his preparation for that existence. Now, instincts are the very reverse of opinions, they are involuntary and intuitive, and indicate a divine presentiment, and the universal instinct of humanity is the anticipation of a future existence; the deniers, if there be any, are an insignificant minority; and when an accepted tradition is in accordance with an equally accepted revelation, it would seem to be the part of prudence, as well as of reason, that we should commit ourselves to "*the larger hope.*"

I began this essay by asking, what am I to do with this unsatisfactory existence? And the answer comes with singular distinctness to my mind. Find out, if you can, its rationale, (and if you will you can); penetrate thoroughly, fearlessly, hopefully into its profoundest depths, and accept what you find there with the confidence of a child and the resolution of a man. Never consent to an equivocation, never employ a sophism, never shrink from the adoption or the avowal or the practical application of a recognized truth. Step by step the solution of the mystery (which can only be reached through the medium of prayer) will unfold itself to your enlarged understanding, and you will find yourself standing upon firm ground, where once you saw nothing but mist and mirage. What has hitherto obscured your vision and encumbered your footsteps is, that you have misunderstood the true order of the universe, and have conducted your investigations under the guidance of Ptolemy rather than of Copernicus. You have exalted sense into a primary element in creation, instead of relegating it to a subordinate position, and have listened to its teachings, as if it were the centre instead of the circumference of your intellectual system; and you have thus deranged the whole process of your mental operations.

Correct the mistake, reverse the order, regard life in its spiritual instead of its natural aspect, and you will find yourself, at once, emancipated from the trammels which now beset you, and poised upon tireless wings in a cloudless empyrean. The array of antagonism which now over-awes you will be brushed aside like the swarming insects of a summer's day, and you will stand, alone if need be, like Perseus in the banquet hall of Atlas, fearless, with the Medusa-head of Truth in your golden satchel.

It is not a hard condition, under which you are required to attain the freedom of *the holy City of God*. No dastard, no trimmer, no halter between two opinions can be admitted there; he would find

himself utterly out of place; he would neither understand the language nor enjoy the intercourse,
nor suit the manners of heroic spirits; he would
still yearn for the diet of falsehood, and gasp for the
atmosphere of corruption, and his baleful presence
would infect the very spirit of love, in which he
would find himself immersed. Moses was required
to take off his shoes upon soil hallowed by the vision
of the burning bush; even the Moslem is not
permitted to enter the temple of his God, without
performing the same reverential ceremony; and the
man, who has attained the beatific vision of truth,
will lift up his heart in gratitude to God, that he
has been required to pass his novitiate through a
night of cold and sleepless vigilance, that he has
been thought worthy to endure a baptism of fire
and to take up his cross with hands washed clean
in the waters of affliction.

Emancipation from the trammels of sense, from
the illusions of falsehood, from the limitations of a
suppository existence is an attainment so far beyond
the reach of our present clouded imagination, that
when it is experienced, we shall only be amazed at

the insignificance of the price at which it has been purchased, and it will add another throb to our emotion of thankfulness, that we have thus been permitted to co-operate in the work of our own liberation. Even here, the spirit of the novice is sometimes so exalted that he can, with entire sin—cerity, adopt the utterance of the ancient martyr, "Ye look for miracles, behold one now, these flames are to me *a bed of roses.*"

To the desert or the cell
Let others blindly fly,
In this evil world I dwell,
Nor fear its enmity ;

Here I find a house of prayer,
To which I inwardly retire ;
Walking unconcerned in care,
And unconsumed in fire.

Good and Evil.

There is no *Evil* in the work of God;
Evil is relative, and a judgment
Of the finite mind, forming a back-ground
To its relative good, and thus confined
To the narrow bounds of our existence,
And offering to man a battle-field
For his struggle upward to perfection.
There is no presence of this human evil
In the mind of God.   When he saw his work,
He pronounced that it was altogether good;
And who shall gainsay what he hath said?
And how could it be otherwise than good?
How could the work of the all-perfect
Be otherwise than perfect, when he spake,
And it was done, and all the sons of God—
The spirits who live in Him, and know His will,
That it is wise and holy, shouted for joy?

Through the veil of matter, through the mask
Of natural change and evolution,
The eye of pure intention and trustful
Observation can recognize and grasp
The blissful end of all ; and those to whom
It hath been given, thus to live in light,
And by sight (not faith) to hold communion
With the eternal mind, from whence all things
Evolve, and to feel, by conscious contact,
The blessedness wrapt up in pain and loss
And sorrow, whence, alone, the soul attains
Self-knowledge—knowledge of the imperfect—
Foreshadowing, by logical converse,
The perfect ; all such have learned to look
Upon this life, with joyful recognition
Of the Creator's hand, turning all evil—
The mortal child of time—to good, which is
Immortal—the essence and evolvement
Of eternity.

What then is Evil,
But an illusive incident, ordained
For purposes divine, in the process

Of a never-ceasing evolution,
Not uncostly, without pain or effort
By the Creative hand, but involving
Labor pains, as of woman in her travail ?
For we do not serve an idle Deity,
A God luxurious or self-centred,
Having no sympathy with His creatures,
Aloof, beyond, above, apart from all
The agony and strife imposed by nature
On her offspring man, cold and calm in his
Unapproachable, serene omnipotence,
Smiling, while he hears the cries ascending
From the tumultuous earth, where misery,
Fear and hate run riot, and where the slave
Of a " vile golden slave*" counts his profit,
Dripping with blood and tears, and vainly deems
Himself the master of the worshippers
Who haunt his palace, ready to lay siege
And sack, when the master-fiend " cries havoc,
And lets slip" the hateful, envious crew
To revel in the immemorial hall

---

*Gold so-called by an East Indian who lost his health in accumulating it.

With hoofs of swine, whose only reverence
Springs from fear, and its fierce offspring, hate.
We serve a God, whose eye takes in the whole,
And governs all, with perfect oversight,
A patient, suffering, Father-God,
In loving sympathy with His children ,
Who bore them on the cross of Calvary,
And bears them on His heart in Paradise.

Good and Evil, as they stand in open
Contradiction, are relative ideas,
Not absolute ; evil is not absolute ;
Good absolute, is God, without *"another*,"
But constituting and embracing all,
The all of life, the all of death, at once
The fountain, the river and the ocean,
The centre and circumference of being.

I have heard, in beautiful similitude,
Creation represented as a Loom,
Whereof the warp and woof were good and ill ;
Producing, by their interchange, nature—
This intangible, invisible all—

A labyrinth, incongruous to man,
But, as seen by the great weaver, perfect
In all symmetrical proportion
And harmony of coloring, evil
Not left to mar the finished pattern,
But purified by elemental fires,
And re-produced in forms of use and beauty.

He who wrote of partial evil as the price
Of universal good, erred from the truth.
There is no partial evil; suffering
Is not evil, but a sacrifice made
To ultimate good, e'en for the sufferer;
And suffering shall last, while the process
Of creative energy shall last,
And God shall be Himself, and the great weaver
Shall produce the ceaseless evolution
Of being, infinite as God Himself.
Let us be content; we yet shall live,
And do the work of God, and find our place
In His eternal universe. So let it be!

What then becomes of punishment eternal?
Shall the Creator, whom we deem just and good,

Punish His frail creature, for being frail;
And that eternally?   Forbid it justice!
Forbid it mercy, and forbid it love!
The letter killeth; not the letter, traced
By Apostolic hand, and sent, as " *Gospel*,"
To a dark, hag-ridden world, yearning
For light, and hoping, against hope, for good;
But the false word, tortured by party zeal,
And wrested from its import, to fulfill
The bitter imprecation of the zealot,
Whose faith, too weak to suffer contradiction,
Could find no place for the dissentient,
But a Hell, constructed in the abysm,
Of terror-stricken conscience, and reserved,
Not for the malignant and despotic soul,
But for the honest and courageous thinker,
Who would not bend to dogmatism, and utter
Words in which he had no faith, and belie.
The Father, whose arms were open to receive
And bless the prodigal, " yet a great way off."

When the Evangelist intends " forever,"
*He uses, not " αιων," but "διηνεκες,"

---

*Pronounced ayone and dienekes.   *Aιων*, Mathew 12. 32.   *Διηνεκες*
Hebrew 10, 12.

As when he says, "sat down, forever,
At the right hand of God ;" but when he says
†" *Αιων*," he speaks, not of Eternity,
But time *measured*, not the immeasurable ;
And thus are reconciled the justice and the love
Of God, now slurred by human orthodoxy.

The mind, which harbors the eternity
Of punishment, impugns the majesty
Of heaven, for it leaves the Creator
In a ruinous dilemma ; either
The Maker is not omnipotent, or
He is not good, and from this alternate
There is no escape, but by a fallacy,
That the Creator hath made one measure
For Himself, another for His creature,
And, therefore, that there is no absolute
Justice, and we float upon an ocean,
Where no pole-star and no compass ensure
The safety of the mariner ; God grant,
That you and I, my Brother, navigate
No such sea, nor fail to find the God-man,

†T*his* α*ιων* and *that* which is to come.

Who hath appeared, that he might make both one ;
One nature, one element and one law ;
And hath introduced us to *our Father* ;
Finite to the infinite united ;
Whereof we find the truth embodied
In that human form, which trod the Syrian hills,
When the time was ripe, and reassured
The orphaned race of Adam that the God,
They ignorantly worshiped, was not he
Who thundered from the riven heights of Sinai ;
Nor Olympian Jove, working his will,
Through subject deities licentious ;
Nor Brama, holding Nirvana as reward
For meritorious self-sacrifice ;
Nor the divided empire of the Median Sage,*
Leaving poor helpless man a shuttle,
Tost, without appeal, between the batons
Of two relentless demons, ruling both
In the chaos of a seething universe.

And was not then the mystery of life,
Revealed, and the high majesty of Truth

*Zoroaster.

Unveiled, when the chains of superstition
Were cast off, and her hereditary slave
Invited to tread, at length, a freeman
In his Father's house ?   This was the message,
And this the truth he came to represent,
And honor, as his synonym, saying
" I am the Truth ;" and he, that loves this Truth,
Hath attained eternal life—the promise,
Which he left, and sealed, forever, with his blood—
And so, may every son of man, who can
Receive and understand the evangel,
Echo back again, " Yea, Lord ! Thou art the truth,
For thou hast shed, upon creation, Light,
Which vindicates Creator, and restores
His creature, wandering, heretofore, through
The dark mountains, orphaned and despairing.

It is not easy thus to read the word,
In the view of that bitter catalogue
Of obstructions, which beset our journey
To the grave, enumerate, with such pathos,
By the world's great Poet.*   It is a tax

*Hamlet's sollloquy.

Upon our courage, to commit ourselves,
Unfalteringly, to the Providence
Of an unseen God, voiceless, obdurate,
Unapproachable through each avenue
Offering itself to an intelligence
Unenlightened by the spirit from above;
And yet, there is no other way to meet
The impenetrable gloom, which o'erhangs
And paralyzes us; we cannot rise
Above ourselves; and, if there is no power
Pledged to our deliverance, then are we
Hopelessly committed to a mortal lot;
" But, I hear the music of celestial
" Harpings; the world is not demoniac
": And dead, a charnel-house, with spectres,
" But God-like, and *my Father's.*" Thus is changed
The whole of life; now am I reconciled;
No! not reconciled, but bound, in joyful
Acquiescence, to life's purifying fires.
Under the influence of a mind enlarged,
I now become inspired by an object
Higher far than happiness, and I bless
The Father of my spirit, that he hath

Made me frail and capable of suffering,
So that the casting of my lot with *good*
May be choice indeed, not a mere consent
To unbought bliss, but a manly sacrifice
Of *self* to the uncompromising claim
Of *Truth* upon the heart and intellect
Of God's highest creature, yet in embryo.
And I most surely do believe, that earth
Affords no happiness, which can compare
With the testimony of our conscience—
That we have identified our being
With Truth and Honor; and thus life's pilgrim
Can joyfully forego earth's satisfactions ;
And the whole philosophy of life,
With all its seeming inconsistencies,
Anomalies and strange fatalities,
To the mind of thoughtful observation,
Is brought within the compass of a word,
And suspends man's destiny upon his *choice.*

We bear a two-fold nature, which demands
An ever-widening nomenclature.
Body and mind, flesh and spirit, life and death,

And, while our temporal *existence*
Depends upon the equipoise of these,
Our real *being* hangs upon the choice
We make between them ; and from that choice
There is no escape ; decline it, and we choose
The lower, and to choose the higher is
To choose relentless sorrow, suffering
To the utmost. Lo ! we have the story,
In the book of Job, traced by a master-hand.
The Almighty Father points the accuser
To his beloved son, in gratified
Approval, saying " Lo ! a perfect man."
" I deny his claim," answers the enemy,
" He hath not been tried." "Try him then," said God
" To the uttermost, but spare his life."
And he was tried, and suffered to the utmost,
And, in many things, he failed, and lost
His perfect trust in God, and the patience
Born of trust, which, among the sons of men,
But *one*, alone, hath perfectly attained ;
But he never lost his hold upon the Rock
Of Ages, or yielded his integrity,
Or relaxed his grasp upon the hand

That guided and sustained him through the maze
Of fierce temptation which assailed him,
Under the sanction of that loving hand ;
And, thus he foiled the tempter, and maintained
His manhood, and vindicated his claim
To an heritage divine, doubly paid.
In a real world, for all he yielded
In the world of shadow, through faithfulness
And confidence in the wisdom of his God ;
For he had trampled on the idol, *self ;*
That portentous idol, which forever
Looms up between us and the Creator
Of our being ; and uttered that sublime
Confession, which, to this day, typifies
All human goodness, "I have heard of thee
" By the hearing of the ear ; but at length
" Mine eye seeth thee.   Wherefore I abhor
" Myself, and repent in dust and ashes."
Thus he silenced the accuser, and stood
Before his Maker, in the spotless robe,
Prepared above for souls that *overcome.*

But, there is a passage in the record,
Which is held as proof unanswerable
That penal suffering must be eternal.
How else can we read the appalling words,
" Where their worm dieth not, and where the fire
" Is not quenched?" Shall we deny the word,
When it contradicts our vain theories?
No; only read the word consistently,
And in accordance with demand of Reason.
For that worm, Remorse, can never die,
And the fire which purifies the soul
Can never mitigate, until creation
Ceases, which is eternal as Creator;
They constitute the anvil and the forge,
By whose efficiency spirits are moulded
In those shapes of beauty and of use,
Which shall be eternal; for all spirits
Are not alike, neither all for beauty,
Nor yet all for use; but all created
To fulfill, each, his allotted function
In the mansion of the great House-holder,
Judged, each, by His standard of perfection.
It is not so with us, who can but judge

By our myopic vision, and remit
Some to honor and some to dishonor,
As may suit our humor or our caprice ;
But all shall there be *recompensed* aright ;
Judgment and mercy meeting in their lot.

This is accordant with the word of truth,
And accordant, also, with the justice
And the love of Him, whose name is *Love.*
And no crude, unscholarly translation,
For whose correctness we have no warrant
But an assumed *authority*, whose power,
Abused, has lost all force with freemen,
Shall e'er entice our feet into those folds,
Whose keepers are no longer shepherds,
Feeding the sheep, and carrying the lambs
Upon their shoulders, as their commissions
Run, but, neglecting the thrice-enforced
Command, measure their worth by a standard,
Not of obedience and humility,
But of worldly dignity and power ;
Not contented with their proper work,

*Corinthians 4.5. Επαινος, not *praise* but *recompense.*

Unless they trample on the conscience
And the intellect of men in all things
Their equals, in many their superiors,
And having prostrated their intellects
Before an orthodoxy, which assumes
To be infallible, demand that all
Bow before their idol, under the threat
Of being heralded, as heterodox,
In the conventicles of the faithful.
Christ has said, "Ask for the holy spirit,"
"To him that asks it shall be given."
This is enough ; rest upon this my brother ;
You will need no other, higher sanction
For your comfort, than those blest words of Christ.

Observe, too, how shamefully unpracticed
In that noble tongue, in which are locked
The records of their faith, are the Rabbis,
Who base their right to rule the conscience
Upon a language wholly out of reach
Of crude and superficial scholarship.
Had they, but once, entered the Shekinah,
And caught a vision of the hidden wealth

Lying, unnoticed, in that ancient crypt,
They would not be held obnoxious
To that criticism, which only deems it
Wasted time to combat their crude errors.

Oh! my Mother, beautiful exceedingly,
And to my loving, reverential eyes
Exhibiting the meek humility
Of the Madonna, I have learned and loved
To follow thee in spirit, not the letter
Which held thy mind enchained, but could never
Mar thy loveliness, or the charity
Which overleaped sectarian hedges,
Oh! my Mother, how often has the thought
Inspired and refreshed my faltering mind,
That, from thy sphere of larger observation
And freer speculation, thou hast marked
The footsteps of thy child, and, by contact
Spirit with spirit, hast interfused
The yearning and the courage, which have made
My mind a glad receptacle of truth;
From thy brave gentleness I have learned
The power of gentleness, and been led,

By the attractiveness of the creature,
To worship and to love the perfect Man,
In whose divine existence was portrayed
That power of weakness, which "led captive
The ravished hearts of men;" and, thus I trust,
That we shall meet again, and live and love,
In him, forever more.

God, in perfect wisdom,
Bends to his purposes that instrument
Which we, in our ignorance, call evil;
But, that the all-wise, all-good, all-mighty
Father should usher into life a soul,
Which he, unable else to utilize,
Should, in revenge, (for what else could it be?)
Consign to never-ending misery,
Is a theory, which no generous
Spirit could e'er originate, and when,
Under the coercion of authority,
It is degraded to the confession
Of such a verbal creed, it must resort
To the employment of a sophism,
Which a mind, unpracticed in the art,

In manly, childlike wisdom, would reject.
And we, my Brother, must become like children,
If we would look upon the face of God.

But the startled ear of dogmatism marks
This threat of danger to its agent, Fear,
And it replies, alarmed, " Shall the rod of Fear
Be henceforth withdrawn from the armory,
Which defends the throne of the world's ruler ?"
Fear is the sole daughter of transgression ;
No sinner ever yet was turned from sin
By power of fear ; fear itself is sin,
The essence and the consequence of sin,
Which only can be turned to holiness
By Love ; for God is Love, and God, alone,
Is power, and the soul, which Love inspires,
Commands that power, which is pledged to Faith ;
The arch fiend retires, abashed, before it,
And fiend-like men, by natural instinct,
Acknowledge it, and shrink from the encounter,
Like him, of old, who fain would wash his hand,
When he delivered up the Just to death.

The soul that fails to realize its ends
Potential, may forfeit, thus, the blessing,
Placed, by a loving hand, within its reach,
Just as a seed, which fails to germinate,
May not attain the glory of a plant;
But neither soul nor seed is without use,
In the economy of creation.
No seed survives the fire, and no soul
Survives the ultimate rejection
Of its highest good; but, in both, there are
Undying elements, which re-appear
In other forms of use and ornament,
Though, what they shall be doth not yet appear.
This is an issue of a mind, arrested
In its onward progress to perfection
By indolence or evil-mindedness.
The intellect, lacking its nourishment,
May wither in its growth, and not attain
The joy and blessedness of life-eternal;
It has preferred a lower consummation.

What then is life eternal? The response
Must come from a higher world; faith knows not;

Sense knows not ; God alone can make reply ;
And the answer comes, in richest measure,
From the God-Man, who was his uttered word.
What saith that word, in parting admonition,
To his chosen few? " This is Life eternal,
That they might know Thee, the only God."
And what is God ? He hath been revealed to us
In no other light than that of Father ;
Christ has said, "*My* Father and *your* Father."
And, thus, we know a friend, whose name is *Love* ;
And, thus, we may approach the infinite!

We all have felt the blessedness, attached
To that benign relation, *Father*,
How it implies the love of parent,
And the care, provision and *protection*,
Patient endurance of our wayward ways,
And all the tender watchfulness, and all
The gentle discipline and firm correction,
Which that name involves, all this, alas !
Marred, in the human, by imperfection ;
Remove, then, created imperfection,
And, thus, give man a Father infinite,

And all that constitutes "*eternal Life*"
Is his, by plain inheritance, forever.

But the mind is still unsatisfied ; it would know
The modus of this wondrous mystery.
How shall imperfect man appropriate
The gift, bestowed so freely ? How attain
Possession of his divine inheritance ?
Let the record speak.   " If ye, being evil,
" Know how to give good gifts unto your child ;
" How much more shall your heavenly Father
" Give the holy spirit *to them that ask* ?"
" *Ask*, and ye shall receive," and, thus, the word
Is vindicated, and its integrity
So sustained, that a little child can read,
Therein, " *The Gospel of our salvation.*"

But, still, the mind is not content with generals ;
It would know the nature of that life
We call eternal ; we can only answer
By negation ; it is, in all respects,
The antithesis of this, it is not
Terrestial life, with death eliminated ;

10

For, if it were, from what, then, are we saved?
To live, forever, in this plague-ridden
World, is that a lot to which we can apply
The glory and the freedom of salvation?
To the sin-wearied soul is death so terrible?
Believe me, that our life, when we awake
From " nature's blest restorer, gentle" death,
Is life indeed, not the poor mockery
Of existence, which deludes us here.
No! no! my Brother, Life, eternal Life
Is not a pitiful toleration,
A cowardly endurance of our fate,
But a condition, energized with might
And the bliss ineffable, which, even here,
Our freed souls anticipate; we bear
That within us, which will not brook delusion ;
And, when the intellect is thus inspired,
It becomes the embryo of a birth
Whose future palingenesis is Love.

All the conditions of that life reject
The transitory and the imperfect,
And all the terms, which are expressive

In the world of time and space, are lame
And inconclusive to the denizens
Of the infinite and eternal world.
Here, we cognize matter with the senses,
There, spirit with spirit holds communion.
Change and decay affect us here below ;
But the condition of that world is *growth*.
Here, we tabernacle in flesh and blood,
There, " in a house, not made with hands,
Eternal in the heavens."

                   England's spoiled poet,
In wanton outbreak of a reckless mood,
Contrasts his human with his canine friend,
And, while ascribing, to his vaunted dog,
Qualities acquired by his life with man,
And, to man, the degradation, which attends
The exclusive culture of his brute nature,
Claims, for the animal, the higher place
In heaven ; and, no doubt, the claim is just,
If by heaven we intend to represent
The gross, voluptuous Paradise
Of that bright, audacious lunatic,

Who gave the world "Don Juan;" but the poor brute
Can never have his part in the true Heaven,
However perfect, in all brute regards ;
For he lacks the element which, alone,
Can fit him to enjoy a higher life.

It is not that he wants intelligence,
Rationality and will ; he enjoys
These functions in inferior measure :
But he is not *conscious* of creation,
And cannot, therefore, cognize a Creator,
And cannot worship what he cannot know.
The animal is not spontaneous
But automatic, and the qualities,
Which we admire as intentional,
Are instinctive, the result of impulse
Which he hath no inward power to resist ;
He cannot apprehend the general term
Which we call *nature*, and which is the mask
Under whose disguise is shown to man
The impersonal infinitude of God.
The difference between the man and brute

*Is generic, they stand not on a level,
And have no ground of fair comparison ;
But all men are worshipers. From highest
Intellect, akin to the seraphic,
To the squalid Bushman, with his fetish,
All men are worshipers, and recognize
A power, which controls their narrow life.
And, herein, is verified the wisdom,
Which propounded, for our admonition,
This proverbial thought, that the tap-root
Of individual character lay
In our estimate of the Creator ;
Whether we regard him as a Father,
To be loved, or a despot, whom we must
Propitiate ; whether we believe him,
When he says, that all is good, or assume
The right to envisage his creation,
According to the crude testimony
Of our imprisoned and imperfect senses.
Once for all, let us surrender ourselves
To the majesty and the might of Him,

*See " *Development*" in "Memoranda and Observations."—This
Volume.

Who made all things from the infinitude
Of his resources.   Some day we shall know.

We have been instructed, with an air
Of kindly patronage, that we must abase
Our Reason before the inspired Word,
Which speaks with an authority divine ;
And so it must be, if they e'er could come
In competition ; But the wise teacher,
In his zeal for self-styled orthodoxy,
Hath failed to read, aright, the record,
Whence he derives his sole authority ;
He hath not, *thus*, interpreted the " Logos,"
That, " In the beginning, there was Reason,
" And Reason was conformity with God,
" And God was Reason; and all things were made
" In conformity with it ; and without it
" Was not anything made that was made."
And, when the Creator gave us *Reason*,
He gave *himself* to us, with conscience
As a sentinel, to warn his creature,
When, under the gloom of superstition
Or the influence of fear, he shall be led

To mistrust his Reason; rather let him hear
The voice within, which comes direct from God,
Than listen to upbraidings from without,
Whether they proceed from Rome, Geneva
Or some popular idol of the hour.

Moreover we have been notified, by those
Who have penetrated the depths of being,
And calculated all the length and breadth,
The depth and height of power that measures
And upholds the world, that eternal life
Is suspended upon unquestioning
Adoption of the dogma, once imposed,
By sectarian vigilance, on the weak,
That, to be fitted for the home of Love,
The surest claim, that mortals can present,
Is the assurance, that the mind of man
Hath analyzed infinity, and resolved
The incomprehensible into a Trinity.*

---

*All the laws of thought compel men to recognize the infinity, and, therefore, the incomprehensibility of the Creator; ambitious spirits are thus cut off from achieving distinction, by a display of their analytic powers in that direction; but, as it is necessary to their self-

Authority hath so decreed, and men
Must bow, not to the God within, the spirit
Promised to them that ask, not to honest,
Heart-felt allegiance to the God-man,
Whose only test was Love, but to the same
Unreasoning authority, which once
Decreed that earth centred the universe,
And condemned the learned man, denying,

---

respect and their assumed intellectual supremacy, that they should exhibit some more intimate acquaintance with the divine nature than the undistinguished multitude, they imagine, that, by furnishing a technical term for the *threefold manifestation* of Deity (a very simple idea and involving no mystery at all), protecting it by an anathema, and heralding it as the result of an analysis beyond the capacity of the common mind, and explanatory of a *mystery*, that they have succeeded in exhibiting a deeper knowledge of the divine nature, than can be attained by the simple, unpretending minds around them. But this is a palpable delusion. No creature can ever comprehend its Creator; the human mind cannot analyze or comprehend the divine nature; as far as such a faculty is possessed, all minds are on a level; we can only know God so far as he reveals himself to us, and the only authentic revelation, that he has made, assures us, not that he is a *Trinity*, but that he is the *Creator, Redeemer* and *Sanctifier* of his rational creatures; the *Father* of our spirits.

Besides this universal revelation, God reveals himself to each individual soul, according to his knowledge of its nature and requirements, and, therefore, no soul is authorized to enforce its own peculiar experiences upon an other.

To the death his bold heresy provoked.
This same *authority* hath goodly marks
Withal, wherewith to brand the recusant,
Casting contempt upon his honest faith,
As the conceited surmise of a fool.
So be it; there are arms open to receive
And welcome wandering fools unto the fold
Of the true Shepherd. Be patient, Oh! my soul.
In our Gospel revelation we can find
No Metaphysic Trinity, cunningly
Devised to circumvent the simple,
And, by a show of just authority,
To persuade the credulous, that the sacred
Name has come, at length, within the grasp
Of the chosen few, who have unveiled
" The mystery of Godliness,"* and that
Henceforth, submitted to the test of mind,
The *essence* of the Deity is analyzed.

The vocabulary of our Evangel
Supplies not to the dogmatist the word,
Which he hath coined for purposes

*Or more properly "God-head."

Of sectarian offense and defense.
There, we find, that the Father of our spirits
Hath *revealed* himself to humanity,
By *three several* manifestations.
We look abroad upon creation,
Mysterious in its origin and end,
And, by *resistless inference*, perceive
The *Maker–God*, Father of our spirits,
Lord of Heaven, Earth and all souls of men.
We desire to impersonate and love
The author of this transcendent work,
And in condescension to our demand
He veils his invisible, essential
Being in *human lineaments*,
Dwelling among men as *perfect man*,
That we may catch the odor of his grace,
And, by contrast, learn to abhor ourselves
And all the ragged righteousness wherewith
We are wont to clothe our imbecility.
But in vain ; Humanity is rotten
At the core, and we need another *heart,*
God-given, God-inspired, to enable us
To resemble and to love Divinity.

And Lo! he comes again, no longer weak,
No longer cumbered by the body,
But, in *spiritual power*, mastering
The citadel of the human heart,
Ejecting thence the traitorous brood
Of carnal passions, and enabling it
To meet the external foe, resistless
With almighty power.*

     And now, you ask
The ground of my belief in the immortal;
And I reply, because it is a part
Of my existence, and an element
Of my construction; I would never know
Where to locate myself, or how account
For my position here, if I were mortal;
It constitutes the furniture and the light,
Which beautify my mind, and which are
The complement and supplement of Life;
And without that faith, God, who is the source
Of being, the centre and circumference

---

*See Archbishop Whately's Logic—Appendix No. 1, clause 19. Subject, *Person.*

Of all that is, would then become, to me,
Only a dark and tantalizing Demon.

Why do I believe in Immortality?
Because I believe in Honor, Truth and Love,
And these are all immortal ; they are
The attributes of God himself, and, thus,
Of sheer necessity, immortal,
And, so far as I find within myself
The germs of these ennobling qualities,
I feel a growing confidence in that
Immortal life, of which they are the types,
The forerunners and constituents.

As the pure mountain air invigorates
And refreshes my material frame,
So am I assured, that an atmosphere
Of Love and Truth will elevate my soul
Unto the higher life ; and, as it is
The lesson of my life-experience,
That, for me, the higher and the lower
Life are incompatible, then I select
That which will survive the wreck of matter ;

And I pay the price most cheerfully ;
For I know, that it is impossible
To apprehend the faintest perfume
Of that higher life, and yet retain
A taste for grosser satisfactions.
Society may not appreciate ;
It may even disapprove ; but Heaven,
(And by that I mean, not Paradise,
Nor any place of sensual enjoyment,
But an internal *state* of Love and Peace)
" Heaven will make amends for all."

MEMORANDA AND OBSERVATIONS.

I am now nearly sixty years old, with a constitution which does not promise many more years of life. An hour of entire stillness tempts me to record, for the benefit of those who accord to me their respect, the result of my experience.

I believe then, without the shadow of a doubt, in a God; and, by that, I mean a being whose attributes are the counterpart of my necessities. In myself, I am nothing, because I am a creature; but a creature implies a creator, and my Creator is equal to all my demands. It is to exhibit and to verify this truth, that my life is constituted as it is. I am not disturbed at the difficulties which attend my probation, because I see clearly, that I could, by no other means, attain a true apprehension of God. It is through the experience of surmounted difficulties, that I gradually learn to understand and trust the inexhaustible resources of the Being who is responsible for my existence.

The forms of expression which suit our relative existence are calculated, I think, to mislead us, when we apply them, as we necessarily do, to our intercourse with our Maker. We speak, for instance, of his forsaking us, of his being angry with us, of his punishing us for our sins; but these are merely figurative expressions and do not accurately represent the attitude of our Maker towards his creatures; that attitude is one of unchanging and ineffable love, which places at our disposal, whenever we choose to make use of it, his infinite power. This fact is the mainspring of the mechanism of human existence. All the interpositions, all the inspirations, all the rebukes and all the encouragements which we encounter in our probationary experience are simply intended to engraft it upon us as an inseparable element of our being. Furnished with this, we become available instruments of divine wisdom and integral elements of divine power. We are able to appropriate the strength which we consciously need for the accomplishment of our superhuman responsibilities. In other words, we are here to be tested, and the whole force of the trial is brought to bear upon one single element of our being —our apprehension of God—and herein, I think, lies the difference between responsible human agents: the varieties of physical, mental and moral power, which they inherit, have no significance in reference to their true being; the important point is, what kind of a God do they worship; and upon the settling of this question their destiny must turn. If they ever come to the limit of the power which they accord to their Deity, or set any bound to his love, a collapse must ensue, which can only be adequately expressed by the word death; there can be nothing left upon which to base their existence or to expend their efforts; if the Creator is circumscribed, what becomes of his creature? But, if my Creator is equal to all the necessities of my being, then, of course, I am immortal; nay more, I am immortally happy; nay more, I am immortally divine.— I live a divine life, I wield a divine power, I enjoy a divine bliss.

What I desire to guard against is the danger at every paroxysm of temptation (probationary life being only a series of temptations), of forgetting, that these paroxysms are the occasions upon which we are

to exhibit the character of our faith. Unless I mis-
understand the language that some persons use in
connection with this word faith, it seems to me that
they have fallen into a serious error in their apprehension of it. Faith in Christ—What is faith in
Christ? To me it seems to be, a conviction that he
has given us a true idea of God, and, in his life and
works, a material exhibition of the mind of God
towards us; that just as no one ever applied to Chris-
for material aid in vain, just as no sorrow, no suffering,
no disease, not even death itself vanquished his love
or resisted his power, so, in matters which concern
our true being, there is no possibility of failure
in the divine provision for our welfare.

I believe, that this is all; the frantic efforts which
some persons seem called upon to make, in order to
give due honor to Christ, the disputes and discussions
and metaphysical subtleties in which they indulge,
in order properly to express their idea of his nature,
his essence, his position in the universe, seem to me
entirely unmeaning and uncalled for.—Christ has no
need of our opinions and our attestations; we cannot
elevate him, nor can we depress him in the scale of

being, but we can attend to him; we can receive his message; we can accept the God that he has revealed to us; and in so doing, we can honor him more, and please him better, than by years of discussions and volumes of litanies.

In other words, I believe that Christ came, not to receive, but to give, not to exact but to confer, not to exalt himself but to bless us; and I cannot conceive of anything, which would come so appropriately as a blessing to creatures constituted as we are, as the assurance that, needy and sinful as we are, we have an infinite Father.—This was his teaching, this was what his life illustrated, and his death confirmed; and upon this I rest my hopes of eternity.

If God is my Father, if I can go to him in my roubles, if I can carry to him my sorrows, my sufferings and my sins, if I can take refuge with him from myself, from my own disturbed and accusing conscience, and from the reproaches of my unhappy fellow sufferers, if, by his very nature, it is impossible for him to turn away or to fail when he undertakes to help me, I do not really see what more I can demand, unless indeed, I shrink from the responsibility of a free will, and decline the glory of immortality—I pre-fer to commit myself to the God whom Christ has revealed to me as his Father and my Father, as his God and my God.

———

I look upon it as a logical necessity, that the Creator of the universe should exercise an infinite and absolute control over his creation, so that nothing can happen therein without his direct agency and uninterrupted energy.

I look upon it as an equally logical necessity, that the result of the creative energy in the development of creation, should be entirely beyond the compre-hension, and, very often, in conflict with the appre-hension of his rational and finite creatures. I consider it equally certain, that the energy of the Creator and its result should be free from *absolute* evil.

And I have the same assurance, that they must involve *relative* evil.

I think, that it also follows, that, as the creature of a *perfect* power, the very best issue that I am capable of experiencing must be in store for me.

I think also, that the present state of existence must be, not a *finality*, but a *nursery*.

Upon these unquestionable convictions rest my present peace and future hope.

Development.

The true doctrine with regard to development, when rightly understood, is simple common science and common sense.

The principles of involution and evolution explain it. They are correlatives.

What is involved in a thing evolves that thing; the two things, however, must be of the same *kind* or *family* or *genus*. The branch *involves* or implies the root; the root *evolves* the branches. Mineral *evolves* vegetable; vegetable evolves animal; animal evolves man. Man *involves* animal, &c. &c.

Man, animal, vegetable, mineral are all genera, and can therefore be correlated; but ape is not a genus but a species, and to correlate it with man is to disregard scientific laws. One kind of ape can involve or evolve another kind; but ape and man cannot be correlated.

To say, that animal involves vegetable is correct science; but to say that animal involves cabbage is unscientific, because one is a genus and the other is a species, and they cannot be correlated.

To say, that man involves animal is correct, because they have generic bodies in common, but to say, that man involves ape, or that ape evolves man is unscientific because one has a generic and the other a specific body and so throughout.

Aristotle points out the mistake, and calls it "slipping over to another kind."

———

The relation of the body to the soul.

It individualizes the soul, gives it form and selfhood; it is the husk or shell in which the soul is sheltered while hardening into concretion—while the various qualities which constitute man are becoming unified and integrated in human form.

The word body, however, needs explanation in this connection. It is not merely the material body, which distinguishes man from his *race*, but it is the composite body (the *me* and the *not—me*, or nature which *constitutes* man, and distinguishes him from his *Creator*), that performs the office of individualizing the soul, and housing it while in its inchoate and tender condition.

When the character is formed and vivified it needs no shelter; on the contrary it requires and demands *to breathe the outer air.*

———

Undoubtedly it is true, that no choice was offered us when we were sent into the world to meet the superhuman difficulties which await us here; no voice that it can comprehend ever whispers to the infant the faintest hint of "the want, the care, the sin," the meanness, the malignity, the treachery, the physical, mental and spiritual agonies which attend its pathway from the cradle to the grave; and our lower nature may well be excused when it seeks, as it will do by this fallacy, to escape from the conscious responsibility which inheres in its diviner element. But the effort must ever be unavailing, as long as that element retains its vitality. There is a voice, low but clear, and audible amidst the infernal din, which says, with no uncertain sound, "meet it all, for you can master it all; he who made you is not only without and around you, checking and quelling the yelping curs which assail you, but, far more, he is within you, a resistless power, defying in its granite strength the fury of a thousand storms."

It is this which vindicates the justice and the love of our Creator; He has panoplied us with His own might, and, while reason and faith give us the promise, our ever accumulating experience gives us the premonition of final and undisputed victory.

———

In matters of principle, never surrender your own judgment; it constitutes your claim to rationality.

———

Remember that you have an *infinite Father* who can protect you, not only against others, which is easy, but against yourself, which is difficult.

———

In your intercourse with your Maker do not *limit* Him.

———

Remember that the power of Christ was typical, and that it extended to the raising of the dead.

Read the Bible and indeed all other books, not to establish adopted views, but to learn the truth.

———

Look well to it that you really desire *truth* at any cost.

———

Avoid censoriousness; commit those whom you think wrong, to God.

———

Never seek to strengthen yourself against another by forming or entering into a combination against him—if you feel tempted to do so mistrust yourself.

———

In a controversy, the only ally you should ever seek is "*truth.*"

———

When foolish or vindictive charges are brought against you, do not be anxious to vindicate yourself. The spirit of truth, which pervades and controls the universe, though an invisible, is an all-powerful vindicator, and resents interference.

Nothing is as high in creation as man, and the highest man is a *child* of God; establish this as a settled principle in your mind, and you will be relieved from the puerilities of ambition.

Remember that office and position mean *duty*, nothing else as far as you are concerned.

In our present state of ignorance and imperfection, it is very difficult to draw the line between a weak compliance with evil and an improper state of mind towards the evil-doer; it will help to clear up the difficulty, to ascertain whether we can honestly ask the same blessing for him that we desire for ourselves. It will, perhaps, also, help us to know the kind of things that we ought to desire for ourselves.

The only real purifier and ennobler is intercourse with God; the moment we recognize human authority either individual or collective, as compulsory in *matters* of *faith*, in matters which concern our intercourse with God, we become emasculated; of course we

11

are bound to recognize human authority in its legitimate sphere.

———

If we do not like an organization we are not bound to enter it; if we do enter it we must conform to its rules—all the laws of society which do not interfere with conscience should be strictly obeyed.

———

I understand the Gospel thus—in the first place I am sure it must be very simple, because it is intended for simple natures, and therefore, all the subtle discussions about it, which have vexed and still vex humanity, are gratuitous, and had better be ignored by earnest minds.

The Gospel comes to *sinners*; tells them that they *are sinners*; that they cannot help themselves, because it is their *nature* to be *sinners*; that God alone can help them; that he does this by taking up his abode *in them*, in the guise of the *Holy Spirit;* and that he will do this *for the asking;* that this course, persevered in, will gradually change their natures, so that they shall be, as it were, born again into a new and holy nature; that this regeneration is a life process; and that all the events of life, if rightly used, will help forward this operation, that the mission of Christ, who was God manifest in the flesh, was to exemplify and declare this Gospel.

My hopes for the future are based upon two unquestionable facts.—That God is—and that He is "my Father."

A proper estimate of *human* (our own) *nature* is perfectly compatible with, nay absolutely necessary to a true love for *human beings.*

Maintain an habitual intercourse with your Maker; you will find in the Creator the reality which the Positivists think they have discovered in the creature.

What is it but our own imperfection which makes it so hard to bear with the imperfection of others?

Yes, my friend! I am, just as you say, a sinner, a proud, foolish, vain, conceited, ignorant sinner, and therefore I cannot go to you for help, who are, by nature, just the same.—"I will arise and go to my Father."

————

Eternal life conditioned upon self–forgetfulness.

The chief cause of our discomfort in this first and lowest stage of existence is owing to an omnipresent and obtrusive little imp, whose importunate demands leave us neither time nor ability to enjoy our magnificent inheritance. This temporary garden of Eden, in which our Creator has placed us, is crowded to overflowing with delights, physical, moral and spiritual so attractive and satisfying, that we naturally dread the thought of leaving them; the poorest and most suffering cling to life with a tenacity which shames and contradicts their discontent, and, if they were left to the free use of their faculties and their instincts, men would find in their humblest surroundings enough to give them occupation and enjoyment, with no other attitude to their neighbours than that of sympathy and good-fellowship; but the busy little imp above alluded to has power to spoil it all. He is able, such is his wonderful influence, to infuse into the cup of life an ingredient so bitter and so pervasive as to neutralize and even counteract the healthy, succulent and luscious elements of which it is composed.

We all know this imp; we cannot help knowing him; for he is our very *self*, bone of our bone and flesh of our flesh; so that we cannot escape from him, as we would from any other annoyance, by resolute avoidance; we cannot bid him depart, for he would rise in mocking exultation and reminded us, that "the Everlasting had set his canon 'gainst self-slaughter." Thus, it is impossible to get rid of our tormentor, and our only hope lies in a compromise—in the acceptance of a divine paradox—we must subsidize the enemy by an appeal to his strongest motives; we must show him that his gain lies in his loss, that his interest depends upon self neglect. How can this be accomplished? I will answer by an illustration.

I once went to hear a very eloquent speaker address an audience upon a very interesting subject; I was late in my attendance and the meeting was already crowded; there was no sitting room and the standing, even by the door, was so packed as to be almost unbearable. I made up my mind, that it could be endured for a very few minutes only. The orator began his address, and I soon saw that he was no common man ; I, at once, became interested and, very soon, entranced ; everything was forgotten, annoyances, fatigue, my surroundings and myself in overpowering enjoyment ; the personal, the subjective, the *me* were entirely lost and overlooked in an external interest which dwarfed them into comparative insignificance.

Here was a hint in the right direction ; if I could forget self temporarily, why not permanently ? If I could lose sight of personal comfort in an intellectual enjoyment, why not in a spiritual one ? If the mind and the voice of a fellow-mortal had the power, thus, to overmaster my subjectivity, what must be the effect of the divine mind and the divine voice upon my spiritual senses, if they could be awakened to the infinite interest which must necessarily be involved in the divine utterances ? Here I think lies the *philosophy* of the paradox.

The practice can only be attained through a divine method, and that method can only be Prayer.

A COLLOQUY.

Who made you?

God.

What is God?

The Spirit of Life.

Perfect or imperfect?

Infinitely perfect.

Are you perfect or imperfect?

Imperfect.

Why were you made imperfect?

In order that my perfection might be an attainment, involving my own coöperation.

What does that coöperation imply?

Rationality.

What is rationality?

Spiritual apprehension, the cognition of cause and effect, the perception of degrees.

What is the field of its exercise?

The moral field.

What do you mean by the moral field?

The field of finite and relative existence, whose component parts are good and evil, right and wrong.

How can God, who is infinitely good, create evil, which is his direct opposite?

He does so relatively, not absolutely.

Explain what you mean by relatively and not absolutely?

As a temporary expedient and not an eternal verity.

What is the object of this *"temporary expedient"*?

That man may exercise the free-will implied in his rationality.

Suppose, then, that, in the exercise of his free–will, man chooses evil and not good?

He forfeits his rationality and lapses into a lower condition of existence.

Can he be happy in this condition?

Not as *man.*

Is he unhappy then?

No, he has only chosen a lower kind of happiness.

Does it not seem to be inconsistent with the divine goodness to give man this fatal power of choice?

Not at all, there are *orders* in creation, and the probationer has chosen that for which he is best fitted ; he was never a real, only a presumptive man.

According to this view then, there is no such thing as *absolute* evil in the universe ?

No, how could there be, if the universe is the creation of a perfect Being ?

How do you reconcile these views with the *letter* of the Gospel ?

The intellectual condition of a soul, that has lost its rationality, is fitly represented by the "the *blackness* of *darkness*," and the passions in which such a soul *delights* are suitably compared to *Hell-fire*.

You maintain that human life is preliminary and probationary, and not a finality ; upon what ground do you form this judgment ?

Its brevity, its uncertainty and its incompleteness ; it is neither symmetrical, nor consistent, nor satisfying.

Are not these indications rather negative than positive ?

They would be, but for the indications of benevolent design which are irresistible.

What are the indications of benevolent design ?

The love of life, which is universal, the actual happiness which exists, and the instinctive anticipation of future good.

If human life, then, is a probation, how are we to know the nature and object of that probation?

By its characteristics.

What are those characteristics?

Its component elements, *good and evil,* and the choice involved in their existence.

Why should such a choice be presented to frail and imperfect intelligences?

It is a necessary attendant upon rationality.

Why should the gift of reason be accompanied by such a test?

It is the only possible proof that the recipient is worthy of the gift.

Would it not have been more benevolent to have saved the delinquents from such an apparently needless ordeal?

I do not see, that it would have been more benevolent to have created them irrational, than to have given them the choice.

What is the fundamental difference between the present and the future states of existence ?

The one is complicated with perishable elements, the other is simple and consequently incorruptible.

What is the relationship between them ?

The one is a shadow—an evanescent type of the other ; the characteristics of the one are change and decay ; those of the other perpetuity and progress.

What do you consider the *actual* condition of those who have forfeited their rationality ?

The term applied in Scripture to their condition is eternal death, which means, I think, the death of their rationality. I think the weight of the testimony goes to establish an *eternal* existence in a *lower state*, with all the satisfactions which that state can afford.

Upon what ground do you express yourself so positively, as to the nature of the present and future states of existence?

Upon the ground of perception ; my senses tell me that matter is mutable, and my understanding assures me, with equal confidence, that Truth and Love are imperishable.

A distinction is commonly drawn between human reason and the divine; what is the difference?

There is really no difference, because there is no such thing as *human* reason; the logical faculty—the power of ratiocination, is the faculty in man through which reason operates, if it is invoked and permitted to act; according to St. John, Reason is the divine power itself.

How do you know that there is any divine power—that there is a Creator?

By the same irresistable conviction that I know that I am a creature; the one involves the other.

May you not be an accidental congeries of faculties—a chance existence?

Chance means chaos; the Cosmos is order; my existence is order, and order implies mind, and unconscious order implies conscious power.

Do you consider the cosmos perfect?

A perfect system of eternal progress.

Progress to what?

To unattainable perfection, typified by those two mathematical lines which are always approaching each other but never coincide.

Why unattainable perfection ?

Because God alone is perfection; creation his eternal work.

Many of the divine requirements are so inconsistent with our human ideas, that it would seem impossible to obey them, except under the influence of a blind and unintelligent faith. Does not the command to love our enemies seem to imply hypocritical pretence?

The command to love our enemies, taken in the literal sense of our very imperfect English translation, not giving the nice distinctions of the Greek vocabulary, would, as you suggest, be very likely to result in hypocricy; but observed with a reasonable, intelligent and sincere intention, and with the proper distinction between the recognition of a common humanity and the attraction of a sympathetic nature, is only what every right minded man would require of himself, if left to the demands of his higher and better nature. The love which the Gospel requires for an enemy is, that we simply apply to him the golden rule, and that we desire for him the same divine compassion and the same wholesome correction which we should wish for ourselves under the same circumstances ; no mawkish, sentimental, fondness ; no impossible personal affection ; but a sincere desire for his true welfare, and an honest committal of his case to one, who loves him more, and knows him better, than we can possibly do : *Love* the antithesis of hate ; *not Love* the synonym of affection.

What do you say to the prohibition of revenge ?

Revenge is prohibited, not as evil in itself, but as unsuited to the narrow comprehension, the unreasoning passions and the selfish instincts of imperfect intelligences : I do not feel that I could be safely entrusted with the power myself, and, as far as I am concerned, I prefer to leave it in the hands of infinite justice and infinite love, where I believe it will be perfectly administered.

But, when that infinite power of which you speak seems to be regardless of the acts of his creatures, and sometimes even to wink at their aberrations, what then ?

Nothing but courageous and consistent confidence in the attributes which reason has assigned to the Creator of the universe; nothing but "patient waiting u on God·"